WARSHIPS
& AUXILIARIES

F229

HMS Lancaster & RFA Gold Rover

THE ROYAL NAVY

The Royal Navy of today has been shaped, over the past five years, by the 2010 Strategic Defence and Security Review, a process driven almost wholly by budgetary requirements rather than an overall strategic or security theme. Wholesale capabilities were either cut completely or gapped, apparently without regard to possible emergent threats, while personnel numbers across all our armed forces were drastically reduced. It is now a matter of record that the Government's contention, at the time, that *"Britain faced no immediate threat to its security or national interests"*, was a seriously flawed assumption.

As a result of SDSR 2010 the intervening years have witnessed the Royal Navy operating at an ever increasing tempo as it tries to cover an ever expanding number of commitments with a vastly reduced pool of ships and personnel. The gapping of fixed wing carrier strike created a major capability shortfall which, despite promises, has not been covered at all effectively by the RAF. Fixed wing carrier operations off Libya were sorely needed and the conduct of air strikes against ISIL in Iraq would have been greatly enhanced had there have been an available carrier. The situation in Ukraine has seen Russia flexing its military muscles - the old enemy might, once again, become a threat we need to counter. At the end of the Cold War the RN had one of the finest anti-submarine fleets in the world. As part of the post Cold War "peace dividend" ASW was no longer considered a high priority and the number of ASW frigates and submarines were greatly reduced. Today Russia is deploying submarines from its northern bases to probe UK defences. With fewer ships and submarines, and with SDSR 2010 axing the replacement Nimrod, no RAF Maritime Patrol capability, the UK now has to call on help from our allies to locate potential Russian incursions around the UK coastline.

Despite having a fleet of just 19 destroyers and frigates, the RN maintains a high tempo of operations as it meets its standing commitments around the World - Operation Kipion sees warships and auxiliaries deployed east of Suez, ensuring peace and stability in the region while at the same time protecting vital trade routes. Maritime trade is still vitally important to the UK economy and industry. 95% of Britain's economic activity depends on the oceans, importing goods worth £524 billion every year; Atlantic Patrol Tasking (North) and Atlantic Patrol Tasking (South) find ships deployed on counter drugs and humanitarian operations in the north to ongoing protection and reassurance to British interests in the south. The number of ships required to cover these deployments puts strain, not only on machinery and equipment, but also on personnel, who find themselves deployed far more frequently and therefore apart from their families for longer periods. The knock on effect is that ships wear out quicker and personnel leave the service.

While the RN is very obviously operating at full stretch, it has always been a "can do" service and continues to take on emergent tasking around the globe - Operation Patwin saw the RN operating in a humanitarian role post Typhoon Haiyan, supporting the Philippines population; Operation Gritrock saw RN helicopters, Medics and Royal Marines deployed onboard the Casualty Receiving Ship RFA ARGUS as they helped in the fight against the Ebola outbreak in Sierra Leone; Triton, an EU Frontex operation, saw BULWARK diverted from the Dardanelles to join the humanitarian operation to counter the migrant crisis in the Mediterranean, later relieved by ENTERPRISE; More recently RICHMOND was diverted from the Gulf to join EUNAVFOR and Operation Sophia as they took the fight to the people smugglers in an attempt to bring to an end the rising tide of human trafficking in the Mediterranean.

Despite the cuts, the high operational tempo and the ever decreasing number of experienced personnel in key sectors, the RN continues to get the job done - but for how long? The RN is facing the double problem of a shrinking fleet which is having to do more and a personnel crisis; seeing senior sailors in key specialities leaving the service for a better, more stable, family life and increased job satisfaction. Recruitment and retention must be addressed, without the right personnel the fleet becomes toothless. Temporary measures such as "borrowing" US Coast Guard engineers to help man the Type 23s is not a long term solution to the problem.

SDSR 2015, which is due to report as this is being written (November 2015), must now start to redress the balance. The 2015/16 Defence Budget is now 2% of GDP at around £35 billion, though this cannot be seen as an increase, encompassing as it does, budgets not previously grouped under the defence vote. However, the Defence Budget is now on firmer foundations with the former financial black holes having disappeared and a substantial surplus being maintained for unseen budget requirements. The challenge for the Government now is to regenerate the UK's military capability while at the same time staying within budget and still meeting the threats likely to be faced in the future. For the RN in particular this will be a challenge as there are several major multi-year equipment programmes underway which will consume large chunks of the equipment budget over a significant period of time.

Part of that new build strategy is already underway. The Astute class submarines are being delivered, albeit very slowly. The small future fleet of just seven Astute class means that the RN is paying a large premium for a bespoke design with a limited production run, exacerbated by the fact that production is being deliberately slowed so that there is no gap in production between the last Astute and the first of the Successor class submarines - the boat intended to replace the four Vanguard class, Trident missile carrying boats. The Successor programme will absorb a large portion of the RN equipment budget for years to come and although long lead items for the proposed four-boat programme have been ordered, the procurement has yet to be debated and approved by the House of Commons.

There is, as there always has been around the issue of nuclear weapons, an ongoing debate as to whether there remains a requirement for a nuclear deterrent and, if such a requirement remains, whether a submarine is the best delivery platform - indeed is there really a need for four boats - many voice the opinion that nuclear tipped cruise missiles could provide the same deterrent value. A very similar debate and very similar arguments preceded the introduction of the Trident armed Vanguard class submarines. Others argue that the UK should not be proliferating its nuclear weapons arsenal - missing the point that the UK has already decreased its holding of nuclear weapons, and that the Successor programme is merely to provide new submarines to carry and launch the existing capability. There can be little doubt that the programme will go ahead - but in what exact form and how many submarines will remain to be seen.

The programme to build two large aircraft carriers, a cornerstone to the Government's declared policy of expeditionary forces, is at last making visible progress. The first ship QUEEN ELIZABETH is nearing the end of her fitting out at Rosyth, while her sister ship PRINCE OF WALES is under construction in an adjacent dry dock. Seeing the first of these put to sea for the first time in 2017 for sea trials will be a milestone in the regeneration of the RN fleet, but it will be many years before either reach their full operational capability. Without doubt they are impressive ships and the fact that the Government have signalled their intention to retain both must be welcomed. However, they remain nothing but large grey boxes until such time as there is a commitment to buy sufficient aircraft to operate from their decks and to ensure a viable fleet structure of destroyers, frigates, Fleet Auxiliaries and submarines to operate with the carrier to form an effective independent Carrier Battle Group. Lacking catapults and arrestor wires these ships will be limited to operating the very expensive, and still untried and still under development, F-35B Lightning. The ships are designed to operate up to 36 such aircraft, but with current estimates suggesting that as few as 48 may be acquired it is difficult to see how they will ever reach their full potential. Given that the aircraft will be jointly operated by the RAF and RN, the carriers will rarely, if ever, deploy with a full wing of 36 aircraft, and even if an operational requirement emerges for such numbers to embark, the cadre of operationally certified carrier trained pilots would preclude such an embarkation without many months of pre-deployment/embarkation training. Proficiency in fixed wing carrier operations necessitates continuous embarkation of aircraft and aircrews, aligned with integration into whole ship operations. Without this hard earned proficiency Carrier Strike will remain nothing more than a desire rather than an actual capability.

The next programme on the horizon is the Type 26 Global Combat Ship, the direct replacement for the Type 23 frigates. The design is nearing maturity and the manufacturing phase is planned to start this year (2016). The stated intention is that the class will be a direct one for one replacement for the earlier ships, but already there is talk of a class of up to 13 vessels. How long before Government start to field the line that the ships are twice as capable as those they replace, therefore we need fewer ships - it is an old political tactic, but one that continues to be employed, despite the counter argument that one ship cannot be in two places at the same time!

Together with the Type 45 destroyer, the Type 26 will form the backbone of the RN escort fleet for several decades to come. This will provide a maximum fleet of just nineteen vessels to cover all deployed standing tasking as well as escort duties to the high value ships and emergent tasks. The migrant crisis in the Mediterranean saw the Prime Minister offer both BULWARK and RICHMOND to support operations. What wasn't declared was that these ships were already deployed on other operations and were detached from those to cover this new tasking.

In an effort to relieve the pressure on these expensive, and complex warships, last year saw an Offshore Patrol Vessel deployed to cover the Atlantic Patrol Ship Task (North), covering the Caribbean and conducting humanitarian and counter narcotics missions. This could be a precursor to seeing the new Batch II Rivers, currently under construction, undertaking such tasking on a more routine basis, thereby releasing a valuable destroyer or frigate to more warfare oriented tasking. The decision to build three new OPVs however, was not taken on operational grounds, but rather to keep the naval shipbuilder busy during the gap in construction between the carriers and the first of the Type 26 frigates. This has also had the knock on effect of changing the specification of the Mine Countermeasures replacement programme which was to have combined the roles of MCM, OPV and survey vessel in one common hull - the OPV role has now been removed from the brief. While little is known of the detail of this future programme it is interesting to note, that within the pages of the 2015 document *UK Defence in Numbers*, produced by the MoD it lists the current MCM, OPV and survey fleet as comprising 42 vessels. Page 9 of this document also gives force numbers for Future Force 2000 - by which time the fleet has reduced to just 24!

The emphasis of SDSR 2010 was to provide the UK with an expeditionary capability - forces able to be moved and deployed rapidly to any part of the world and, once there, able to fight and be supported from the air and sea. Key to this are the RNs amphibious forces. Largely neglected since the end of the Cold War, new investment saw the commissioning of a helicopter carrier, two LPDs, four Bay class LSDs operated by the RFA and six merchant manned Ro-Ro vessels. However, already, these assets have been depleted. Two of the Ro-Ros have been sold as no longer required. One of the LSDs has been sold to Australia and the remaining vessels are either used for non-amphibious roles (MCM support in the Gulf and humanitarian operations in the Caribbean) or simply laid up. One of the two LPDs is kept in reserve and OCEAN is nearing the end of its life with no plans to replace her.

The Response Force Task Group (RFTG) is the Royal Navy's expeditionary task force maintained at high-readiness and available at short notice to respond to unexpected global events. It is exercised each year under the Cougar series of deployments but to date these operations are yet to demonstrate a fully integrated and operationally deployable combat formation. RFTG rarely deploys with a full RN escort screen, submarine assets or complete Air Groups. Again, it appears that this capability is a desire rather than a reality.

The Government is keen to remind us that the UK has the fifth largest defence budget. That however, is meaningless if money is not being spent wisely. The current build plan and force structure outlined in the preceding pages shows an abundance of high value programmes and bespoke "gold standard" warships built at a premium to support UK shipbuilding and to maintain a sovereign capability in the defence building sector - essential, according to the Government, as in time of conflict we cannot be sure who our allies will be or whether it would be possible to maintain supply of essential spares and equipment. However, this flies in the face of the Government's other contention that we don't need to have fully rounded forces capable of fielding every military capability as, in time of conflict, we can rely on our allies to fill such gaps as maritime patrol or airborne electronic warfare; or to plug gaps in our escort forces or provide replenishment services. So, we must maintain our sovereign shipbuilding infrastructure as we don't know who our allies might be but, we can gap or dispense with critical military capabilities as we do know who our allies will be.

SDSR 2015 must match political will and funding to military and security requirements. Shipbuilding has to provide better value for money. Is it time for a sea change in the way we order warships? Bespoke vessels from a single supplier in small quantities is too expensive. Why not buy 'off the shelf', there are plenty of good designs out there. Or build some classes to merchant ship standards – HMS OCEAN has, by and large, been a successful and relatively inexpensive platform which has performed well since 1995, albeit slower than we might wish?

The desire to build new vessels must be matched by a parallel effort to recruit sufficient manpower, to man, maintain and operate these assets - and more importantly to ensure that terms of service and remuneration are sufficiently attractive to retain them in service - without the necessary manpower, ships, no matter how few, how many or how powerful, will never go to sea.

There must also be a move away from headline grabbing announcements of new orders, only to find a few years down the line that they were just that - announcements, and that contracts had not been placed. The F-35B is a case in point – The Ministry of Defence should commit to the numbers required and agree a schedule for acquisition and introduction into service.

It is too much to hope that SDSR 2015 will contain anything concrete in way of orders or future equipment but one thing is sure - there is no more money to be had, so that which is in the budget must be spent more effectively. Unlike SDSR 2010 the Government must now be alert to the fact that there are immediate threats to the security of the UK - recent events in Paris have shown how quickly and violently such threats can strike. With a credible capability comes effective deterrence and threat. The UK needs to be ready to respond to all threats, from wherever they may come - and that means having a fully rounded military capability ready to deter, counter, or react to all or any groups or nations that may wish us harm.

Steve Bush
Plymouth, 2015

SHIPS OF THE ROYAL NAVY
Pennant Numbers

Ship	Pennant Number	Page	Ship	Pennant Number	Page
Assault Ships			VIGILANT	S30	9
			VENGEANCE	S31	9
OCEAN	L12	13	TORBAY	S90	12
ALBION	L14	14	TRENCHANT	S91	12
BULWARK	L15	14	TALENT	S92	12
			TRIUMPH	S93	12
Destroyers			ASTUTE	S119	10
			AMBUSH	S120	10
DARING	D32	15	ARTFUL	S121	10
DAUNTLESS	D33	15			
DIAMOND	D34	15	**Minehunters**		
DRAGON	D35	15			
DEFENDER	D36	15	LEDBURY	M30	19
DUNCAN	D37	15	CATTISTOCK	M31	19
			BROCKLESBY	M33	19
Frigates			MIDDLETON	M34	19
			CHIDDINGFOLD	M37	19
KENT	F78	17	ATHERSTONE	M38	19
PORTLAND	F79	17	HURWORTH	M39	19
SUTHERLAND	F81	17	QUORN	M41	19
SOMERSET	F82	17	PENZANCE	M106	21
ST ALBANS	F83	17	PEMBROKE	M107	21
LANCASTER	F229	17	GRIMSBY	M108	21
ARGYLL	F231	17	BANGOR	M109	21
IRON DUKE	F234	17	RAMSEY	M110	21
MONMOUTH	F235	17	BLYTH	M111	21
MONTROSE	F236	17	SHOREHAM	M112	21
WESTMINSTER	F237	17			
NORTHUMBERLAND	F238	17	**Patrol Craft**		
RICHMOND	F239	17			
			EXPRESS	P163	25
Submarines			EXPLORER	P164	25
			EXAMPLE	P165	25
VANGUARD	S28	9	EXPLOIT	P167	25
VICTORIOUS	S29	9	CLYDE	P257	23

Ship	Pennant Number	Page	Ship	Pennant Number	Page
ARCHER	P264	25	PUNCHER	P291	26
BITER	P270	25	CHARGER	P292	26
SMITER	P272	25	RANGER	P293	26
PURSUER	P273	25	TRUMPETER	P294	26
TRACKER	P274	25			
RAIDER	P275	25	**Survey Ships & RN**		
BLAZER	P279	25	**Manned Auxiliaries**		
DASHER	P280	25			
TYNE	P281	22	GLEANER	H86	29
SEVERN	P282	22	ECHO	H87	28
MERSEY	P283	22	ENTERPRISE	H88	29
SCIMITAR	P284	24	SCOTT	H131	27
SABRE	P285	24	PROTECTOR	A173	30

HMS Victorious

SUBMARINES
VANGUARD CLASS

Ship	Pennant Number	Completion Date	Builder
VANGUARD	S28	1992	VSEL
VICTORIOUS	S29	1994	VSEL
VIGILANT	S30	1997	VSEL
VENGEANCE	S31	1999	VSEL

Displacement 15,980 tons (dived) **Dimensions** 149.9m x 12.8m x 12m **Speed** 25 + dived **Armament** 16 Tubes for Trident 2 (D5) missiles, 4 Torpedo Tubes **Complement** 135

Notes

After the first successful UK D5 missile firing in May '94 the first operational patrol was carried out in early '95 and a patrol has been maintained constantly ever since. The UK's Trident missiles have been de-targeted since 1994, and the submarine on deterrent patrol is normally at several days notice to fire her missiles. Due to delays in the Successor submarine programme, the service life of the Vanguard class has been extended to beyond 2028 while at the same time reducing the number of operational missiles on each submarine to just eight. To achieve this five year extension three additional Long Overhaul Periods (LOPs) will be required, at Devonport, costing around £1.3 billion between 2014 and 2024. It is anticipated that once VENGEANCE completes her refit VANGUARD will re-enter the refit cycle at the end of 2015. A decision on refuelling VICTORIOUS will follow in 2018.

DANIEL FERRO

HMS Ambush

ASTUTE CLASS

Ship	Pennant Number	Completion Date	Builder
ASTUTE	S119	2009	BAe Submarine Solutions
AMBUSH	S120	2012	BAe Submarine Solutions
ARTFUL	S121	2015	BAe Submarine Solutions
AUDACIOUS	S122	2018	BAe Submarine Solutions
ANSON	S123	2020	BAe Submarine Solutions
AGAMEMNON	S124	2022	BAe Submarine Solutions
AJAX	S125	2024	BAe Submarine Solutions

Displacement 7,400 tonnes (7,800 dived) **Dimensions** 97m x 11.2m x 9.5m **Speed** 29+ dived **Armament** 6 Torpedo Tubes; Spearfish torpedoes; Tomahawk cruise missiles for a payload of 38 weapons **Complement** 98 (Accommodation for 12 Officers and 97 Ratings)

Notes

Ordered in 1997, the Astute class will replace the Trafalgar class in RN service. AMBUSH was commissioned on 1 March 2013, having arrived at Faslane on 19 September 2012. The third boat ARTFUL was launched on 19 May 2014 and conducted her first basin dive on 7/8 October. She sailed from Barrow on 13 August 2015 for sea trials, arriving at Faslane a week later. AUDACIOUS will be the first to benefit from a so-called Design for Cost Reduction initiative, a redesign activity pursued by BAE Systems, the MoD and its key suppliers to ensure the affordability of later boats, addressing both the platform and combat system. As well as re-engineering certain parts of the original design, there was a move to commercial-off-the-shelf systems for some of the combat system equipments.

All major fabrications for ANSON are now complete and awaiting assembly. The keel ring for the sixth submarine, AGAMEMNON, was ceremonially laid down on 18 July 2013. The seventh submarine, AJAX*, has been confirmed, but not yet ordered.

The Astute class is designed to fulfil a range of key strategic and tactical roles including anti-ship and anti-submarine operations, surveillance and intelligence gathering and support for land forces. Each boat will have a lock in lock out capability, enabling swimmers to leave the submarine while dived. This capability is in addition to the Chalfont dry deck hangar which can be fitted to the aft casing and designed to hold a swimmer delivery vehicle for stand off insertion.

The planned in-service dates for the remainder of the Astute class boats are: AUDACIOUS (2018); ANSON (2020); AGAMEMNON (2022) and AJAX (2024).

*There is some confusion as to whether or not the seventh boat will be named AJAX. The name has been associated with the Astute class for some years and has appeared both in print and on the RN website, but this has now been removed. Whether or not the name was released unofficially or has fallen out of favour is unknown, but at present neither the MoD nor BAE refer to the vessel as anything other than Hull 7.

HMS Astute with Chalfont Dry Deck shelter. The aft section of conning tower fairing is removed to allow embarkation of the shelter. (Daniel Ferro)

HMS Torbay

TRAFALGAR CLASS

Ship	Pennant Number	Completion Date	Builder
TORBAY	S90	1986	Vickers
TRENCHANT	S91	1989	Vickers
TALENT	S92	1990	Vickers
TRIUMPH	S93	1991	Vickers

Displacement 4,500 tons 5,200 tons dived **Dimensions** 85.4m x 9.8m x 9.5m **Speed** 30+ dived **Armament** 5 Torpedo Tubes; Spearfish torpedoes; Tomahawk cruise missiles for a payload of 24 weapons **Complement** 130

Notes

TORBAY, TALENT, TRENCHANT and TRIUMPH have undergone upgrade and received Type 2076 Sonar. Beginning in 2014 the final four submarines began a communications package upgrade to overcome obsolescence issues. With delays to the Astute class, decommissioning dates for the remaining T class have been extended. In 2015 TRIUMPH underwent an eight month refurbishment programme at Faslane while TRENCHANT neared completion of a Revalidation and Maintenance Period (RAMP) at Devonport. In December 2014 TALENT returned to Devonport for repairs to her conning tower after sustaining damage in what the MoD referred to as "a collision with floating ice". Following temporary repairs the submarine resumed her deployment, returning to Devonport in March 2015. The four boats are scheduled to decommission as follows: TORBAY (2017); TRENCHANT (2019); TALENT (2021) and TRIUMPH (2022).

LANDING PLATFORM HELICOPTER OCEAN

Ship	Pennant Number	Completion Date	Builder
OCEAN	L12	1998	Kvaerner

Displacement 22,500 tonnes **Dimensions** 203.8m x 35m x 6.6m **Speed** 17 knots **Armament** 3 x Phalanx, 4 x 30mm ASC guns, 4 x Minigun **Aircraft** Tailored Air Group (Merlin, Sea King, Chinook, Apache as required) **Complement** Ship 285, Squadrons 206 (maximum 1275 including Royal Marines)

Notes

Can carry 12 Sea King and 6 Lynx helicopters. RAF Chinook helicopters are normally carried as an integral part of the ship's air group, but they are unable to be stowed below decks. Vessel is somewhat constrained by her slow speed. Many improvements have been made to her including accommodation for both crew and embarked Royal Marines; advanced communications facilities; a better weapon defence system and an upgrade to the ship's aviation support facilities to improve support to helicopter operations including the Apache attack helicopter. She completed a 15-month refit at Devonport in July 2014. Major upgrades included the installation of Type 997 (Artisan) radar and the replacing of the 20mm guns by four 30mm Automated Small Calibre gun systems. In 2015 she participated in Baltops, Joint Warrior and the annual Cougar deployment. Papers placed in the House of Commons Library reveal the ship is due out of service in 2019 without replacement.

HMS Bulwark

LANDING PLATFORM DOCK

ALBION CLASS

Ship	Pennant Number	Completion Date	Builder
ALBION	L14	2003	BAe Systems
BULWARK	L15	2004	BAe Systems

Displacement 18,500 tons, 21,500 tons (flooded) **Dimensions** 176m x 25.6m x 7.1m
Speed 18 knots **Armament** 2 x CIWS, 2 x 20mm guns (single) **Complement** 325
Military Lift 303 troops, with an overload capacity of a further 405

Notes

Vehicle deck capacity for up to six Challenger 2 tanks or around 30 armoured all-terrain tracked vehicles. Floodable well dock able to take four utility landing craft. Four smaller landing craft carried on davits. Two-spot flight deck able to take medium support helicopters and stow a third. Flight deck allows the simultaneous operation of two Chinook helicopters. These vessels do not have a hangar but have equipment needed to support aircraft operations. Only one of the class remains operational at this time. BULWARK assumed the role of fleet flagship in October 2011. In April 2015 she was diverted from the Dardenelles to conduct humanitarian and search and rescue operations in the Mediterranean during the migrant crisis, returning to Devonport in July. In 2012 ALBION entered a 33-month period of extended readiness at Devonport. In December 2014 ALBION entered dry dock at the start of her 2½ year-long regeneration refit. She is expected to rejoin the fleet in April 2017 at which time BULWARK will be laid up at extended readiness.

HMS Defender

DESTROYERS
DARING CLASS
(Type 45)

Ship	Pennant Number	Completion Date	Builder
DARING	D32	2008	BVT Surface Fleet
DAUNTLESS	D33	2008	BVT Surface Fleet
DIAMOND	D34	2009	BVT Surface Fleet
DRAGON	D35	2011	BVT Surface Fleet
DEFENDER	D36	2012	BVT Surface Fleet
DUNCAN	D37	2013	BVT Surface Fleet

Displacement 7,350 tons **Dimensions** 152.4m x 21.2m x 5.7m **Speed** 29 knots **Armament** 1 - 4.5-inch gun, 2 x Quad Harpoon missile launchers (on four ships), Sea Viper missile system comprising Sylver VLS with combination of up to 48 Aster 15 and Aster 30 missiles, 2 x Vulcan Phalanx (fitted as required) **Aircraft** Lynx or Merlin **Complement** 190 (with space for 235)

Notes

Originally to have been a class of "up to" 12 ships this was reduced to just six. DRAGON was the first of the batch two destroyers, which include upgrades to systems onboard in line with technological developments.

The MoD have acknowledged that the ships have had some equipment reliability issues, which was to be expected with a new class of warship. However the majority of those have been resolved and work is continuing to address those that remain outstanding. The cost is being funded from within the existing MoD equipment support budget. On the specific issue of the ships' power and propulsion system the MoD have identified a number of issues that can be addressed in the short term and are making progress in resolving them. The MoD is also considering making improvements, through upgrades, to the diesel generators, with a view to adding greater resilience to the class by increasing electrical generation capacity. The feasibility phase for this work, which was co-funded by BAE Systems and the MoD, concluded at the end of March 2015 and the outputs from this are currently being reviewed. A decision on whether to proceed with the upgrade programme will then be considered against wider defence priorities and if taken forward, would be funded by the MoD.

The ships are capable of contributing to worldwide maritime and joint operations in multi threat environments and are primarily air defence ships. The Sea Viper missile ensures that the ships can destroy incoming threats from the air whilst the Sampson Multi-Function Radar can simultaneously detect and track over four hundred targets, providing a fully automatic operation where rapid reaction is required. In 2013 DARING participated in an anti-ballistic missile exercise with the US Navy in the Pacific to prove the Sampson radar in that mode. Although there are no plans to field an ABM missile, funding has been provided to demonstrate Sampson running ABM and AAW functions simultaneously.

In order to give the ships an anti-ship capability the Harpoon missile systems removed from the decommissioned Batch III Type 22 frigates are being fitted to four of the Type 45 destroyers. DUNCAN was the first to go to sea with the system fitted.

The Harpoon installation on HMS DUNCAN, mounted between bridge and Sylver VL silos.
(Daniel Ferro)

In June 2014 the MoD awarded BAE Systems a £70 million contract to manage the support, maintenance and upgrade of the Type 45 destroyers at Portsmouth Naval Base and on all their operations, both in the UK and globally.

HMS Monmouth

FRIGATES
DUKE CLASS (Type 23)

Ship	Pennant Number	Completion Date	Builder
KENT	F78	2000	Yarrow
PORTLAND	F79	2000	Yarrow
SUTHERLAND	F81	1997	Yarrow
SOMERSET	F82	1996	Yarrow
ST ALBANS	F83	2001	Yarrow
LANCASTER	F229	1991	Yarrow
ARGYLL	F231	1991	Yarrow
IRON DUKE	F234	1992	Yarrow
MONMOUTH	F235	1993	Yarrow
MONTROSE	F236	1993	Yarrow
WESTMINSTER	F237	1993	Swan Hunter
NORTHUMBERLAND	F238	1994	Swan Hunter
RICHMOND	F239	1994	Swan Hunter

Displacement 4,900 tonnes **Dimensions** 133m x 16.1m x 5m **Speed** 28 knots **Armament** Harpoon & Seawolf missile systems: 1 - 4.5-inch gun, 2 - single 30mm guns, 4 - 2 twin, magazine launched, Torpedo Tubes, Lynx or Merlin helicopter **Complement** 185

Notes

Now the sole class of frigate in RN service, the ships incorporate 'Stealth' technology to minimise magnetic, radar, acoustic and infra-red signatures. Gas turbine and diesel electric propulsion. Type 2087 Sonar is to be fitted in only 9 of the remaining 13 of the class (ARGYLL, MONTROSE, MONMOUTH and IRON DUKE will not receive the upgrade). MONTROSE is in refit until 2016.

In August 2008 the MoD announced that the Type 996 surveillance and target indication radar was to be replaced by the ARTISAN 3D Medium Range Radar (now designated Type 997) under a £100 million contract covering demonstration, manufacturing, delivery and the first 10 years of in-service support. The ARTISAN 3D (Advanced Radar Target Indication Situational Awareness and Navigation) is a modular open architecture maritime radar system designed to deal with complex littoral environments. It is being incrementally installed from 2011 as part of the Capability Sustainment Programme (CSP). The Seawolf missile system is expected to reach the end of its service life around 2018 and will be replaced by the Sea Ceptor between 2015-2021. In June 2015 ARGYLL began a docking period at Devonport, the first of class to undergo a LIFEX refit bringing together CSP and extending the life of the hull and supersturcture. She will be the first of class to receive the Future Local Area Air Defence System (FLAADS), or Sea Ceptor, replacing Sea Wolf as the primary weapon system.

In 2014 Babcock was awarded a contract to deliver an off-the-shelf Communications Electronic Support Measures (CESM) system to provide an enhanced electronic surveillance capability. The system, Hammerhead, will provide surveillance capability, supporting both tactical indicators and warnings and other tasked requirements. Babcock teamed with principal subcontractor Argon ST to deliver a system requiring no development work, to enable rapid replacement of the existing obsolete system on the Type 23s.

The MoD has also begun procurement activity to upgrade the power generation system, switchboards and machinery control and surveillance systems under the Power Generation and MCAS Update programme. On 7 August 2015 the MoD awarded a £68M contract, to Rolls-Royce subsidiary MTU, which includes a training and transitional support package which will see each ship supplied with four new diesel generators and associated upgraded power distribution. A second contract, worth £12 million, went to Hitzinger UK, to provide voltage converters to deliver greater power to the frigates.

Currently, ships are scheduled to decommission as follows: ARGYLL (2023); LANCASTER (2024); IRON DUKE (2025); MONMOUTH (2026); MONTROSE (2027); WESTMINSTER (2028); NORTHUMBERLAND (2029); RICHMOND (2030); SOMERSET (2031); SUTHERLAND (2033); KENT (2034); PORTLAND (2035) and ST. ALBANS (2036).

HMS Middleton

MINE COUNTERMEASURES SHIPS (MCMV)
HUNT CLASS

Ship	Pennant Number	Completion Date	Builder
LEDBURY	M30	1981	Vosper T.
CATTISTOCK	M31	1982	Vosper T.
BROCKLESBY	M33	1983	Vosper T.
MIDDLETON	M34	1984	Yarrow
CHIDDINGFOLD	M37	1984	Vosper T.
ATHERSTONE	M38	1987	Vosper T.
HURWORTH	M39	1985	Vosper T.
QUORN	M41	1989	Vosper T.

Displacement 750 tonnes **Dimensions** 60m x 10.5m x 3.4m **Speed** 15 knots **Armament** 1 x 30mm + 2 x Miniguns **Complement** 45

Notes

The largest warships ever built of glass reinforced plastic. Their cost (£35m each) has dictated the size of the class. Very sophisticated ships - and lively seaboats! All are based at Portsmouth as the Second Mine Countermeasures Squadron (MCM2).

BAE Systems has been awarded a six-year contract worth £15m to replace the propulsion systems on these ships, with the work to be carried out at Portsmouth. The first new propulsion system, comprising two Caterpillar C32 engines (replacing the older Napier Deltics) has been installed on board CHIDDINGFOLD. Upgrades to the remaining seven ships will take place during planned ship docking periods up to 2016. The re-propulsion project will involve the installation of new engines, gearboxes, bow thruster systems, propellers and machinery control systems. In September 2015 Crew 3 of the Second Mine Countermeasures Squadron took responsibility for BROCKLESBY, as she is prepared for a dry-dock refit period, during which time she will undergo an extensive overhaul including a complete replacement of her propulsion plant. She is due to return to the fleet in late 2016.

In order to keep up the overseas deployment tempo, crews are swapped between ships. ATHERSTONE and CHIDDINGFOLD are forward deployed to the Gulf. QUORN returned to the UK in September 2014 after three years in the Gulf, having been replaced by CHIDDINGFOLD which left Portsmouth in June 2014. MIDDLETON sailed from the UK on 9 November 2015 to replace ATHERSTONE.

In 2013 the 9th MCM Squadron was stood up at Bahrain, comprising those vessels deployed to the Gulf in support of mine countermeasures operations. Those ships will be identified by a squadron funnel emblem depicting a traditional dhow, resurrecting the identity of the Ton class vessels deployed to the Gulf in the 1960s and 1970s as 9th MSS and latterly 9th MCMS.

Published decommissioning dates are LEDBURY (2019), CATTISTOCK, BROCKLESBY, CHIDDINGFOLD and MIDDLETON (2020), HURWORTH and ATHERSTONE (2022) and QUORN (2023). This is at odds with a press release from the RN on MIDDLETON's return to service in 2014 following her refit and diesel replacement. It was stated that the new engines mean that MIDDLETON can sail faster, stay at sea longer, and will extend the ship's life to 2030 and beyond.

As part of the wider Mine Countermeasures Hydrographic (MHC) programme – intended to deliver a replacement for the RN's mine warfare and hydrographic capabilities – the so-called MHC Sweep Capability project plans the introduction of a new remote control minesweeping system for deployment from the Hunt class, which lost its minesweeping capability when the sweep wires and associated equipment were removed in 2005. HAZARD, an optionally manned surface craft that will be able to venture into minefields to launch and recover unmanned underwater vehicles to search, locate and dispose of mines, can also be used to tow combined influence sweep gear. The concept is being tested by the Maritime Autonomous Systems Trials Team (MASTT) around Portsmouth. It is ultimately envisaged that a full scale demonstration, in the 2018-19 timeframe, could see a Hunt class converted for the launch and recovery of such vessels via an 'A' frame at the stern.

HMS Bangor

SANDOWN CLASS

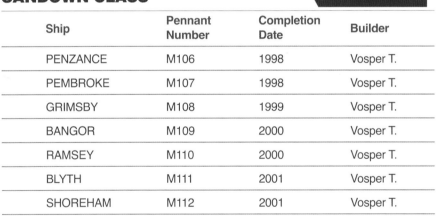

Ship	Pennant Number	Completion Date	Builder
PENZANCE	M106	1998	Vosper T.
PEMBROKE	M107	1998	Vosper T.
GRIMSBY	M108	1999	Vosper T.
BANGOR	M109	2000	Vosper T.
RAMSEY	M110	2000	Vosper T.
BLYTH	M111	2001	Vosper T.
SHOREHAM	M112	2001	Vosper T.

Displacement 600 tons **Dimensions** 52.5m x 109.m x 2m **Speed** 13 knots **Armament** 1 - 30mm gun; 2 x Miniguns; 3 x GPMG **Complement** 34

Notes

A class dedicated to a single mine hunting role. Propulsion is by vectored thrust and bow thrusters. All are based at Faslane as the First Mine Countermeasures Squadron (MCM1). The ships are manned by eight numbered crews which are rotated throughout the squadron allowing deployed vessels to remain on station for extended periods. PENZANCE and BANGOR are forward deployed to the Gulf, SHOREHAM having returned to the UK in August 2015.

HMS Severn

PATROL VESSELS
RIVER CLASS

Ship	Pennant Number	Completion Date	Builder
TYNE	P281	2002	Vosper T.
SEVERN	P282	2003	Vosper T.
MERSEY	P283	2003	Vosper T.

Displacement 1,677 tonnes **Dimensions** 79.5m x 13.6m x 3.8m **Speed** 20+ knots
Armament 1 x 20mm; 2 x GPMG **Complement** 48

Notes

Ordered on 8 May 2001, the deal was unusual in that the ships were leased from
Vospers (VT) for five years under a £60 million contract. In January 2007 a £52 million
lease-contract extension was awarded extending their RN service to the end of 2013.
In September 2012 Whitehall signed a £39m contract to buy the ships outright, keep-
ing them in service with the RN for the next ten years. The River class are now the only
RN ships permanently conducting Fishery Protection patrols in the waters around
England, Wales and Northern Ireland. In the autumn of 2014 SEVERN deployed to the
Caribbean to take over the Atlantic Patrol Task (North), the first time an OPV has been
deployed on this operation. She returned to the UK in July 2015. It is likely that this was
a 'concept proving' deployment in advance of the new Batch II River class entering service. It has still not been determenined whether the class will remain in service once
the Batch II River class are completed (see page 44).

HMS Clyde

BATCH II RIVER CLASS

Ship	Pennant Number	Completion Date	Builder
CLYDE	P257	2006	VT Shipbuilding

Displacement 1,847 tonnes **Dimensions** 81.5m x 13.6m x 4.15m **Speed** 19 knots (full load) 21 knots (sprint) **Aircraft** Flight Deck to take Lynx, Sea King or Merlin Helicopter **Armament** 1 - 30mm gun; 5 x GPMG; 2 x Minigun **Complement** 36 (space for additional 20 personnel - see note)

Notes

Designed to carry out patrol duties around the Falkland Islands and their dependencies, the ship is able to accommodate a single helicopter up to Merlin size. She deployed to the Falklands in August 2007. CLYDE's more modern design has enabled her to remain on task in the South Atlantic until later this year. Like the previous River class, she had been leased from BAE Systems, for a period of five years. In July 2011 it was announced that BAE Systems had been awarded a six-year contract extension to deliver support services to the ship until 2018. The annual cost to the public purse of operating the ship is £3.5 million.

CLYDE is able to embark a Military Force of up to 110 personnel (the size of the Roulement Infantry Company (RIC)) and move them around the Falkland Islands, inserting them at will.

HMS Sabre

SCIMITAR CLASS

Ship	Pennant Number	Completion Date	Builder
SCIMITAR	P284	1988	Halmatic
SABRE	P285	1988	Halmatic

Displacement 18.5 tons   **Dimensions** 16m x 4.7m x 1.4m   **Speed** 27+ knots
Armament 2 x GPMG **Complement** 4

Notes

Assigned to the Royal Navy Gibraltar Squadron (RNGS) the vessels provide Force Protection to visiting coalition warships, maritime security patrols within British Gibraltar Territorial Waters and support a variety of operations within the Joint Operating Area. In recent years the craft have been facing increasingly provocative stand-offs with their Spanish counterparts in the Guardia Civil as Spain tries to assert its influence over, what it views as, disputed waters in the Bay of Gibraltar. In response additional RN personnel have been deployed to Gibraltar, increasing the number of crews from two to three. RNGS also operate up to three Rigid Hull Inflatable Boats supported by two 15 metre launches and three Arctic 24 RHIBS operated by the Gibraltar Defence Police.

HM Ships Pursuer, Biter & Explorer

COASTAL TRAINING CRAFT
P2000 CLASS

Ship	Pennant Number	Completion Date	Builder
EXPRESS	P163	1988	Vosper T.
EXPLORER	P164	1985	Watercraft
EXAMPLE	P165	1985	Watercraft
EXPLOIT	P167	1988	Vosper T.
ARCHER	P264	1985	Watercraft
BITER	P270	1985	Watercraft
SMITER	P272	1986	Watercraft
PURSUER	P273	1988	Vosper T.
TRACKER	P274	1998	Ailsa Troon
RAIDER	P275	1998	Ailsa Troon
BLAZER	P279	1988	Vosper T.
DASHER	P280	1988	Vosper T.

Ship	Pennant Number	Completion Date	Builder
— PUNCHER	P291	1988	Vosper T.
CHARGER	P292	1988	Vosper T.
RANGER	P293	1988	Vosper T.
TRUMPETER	P294	1988	Vosper T.

Displacement 54 tonnes **Dimensions** 20m x 5.8m x 1.9m **Speed** 20 knots **Armament** 3 x GPMG (Faslane based vessels) **Complement** 5 (with accommodation for up to 12 undergraduates).

Notes

Fourteen P2000 craft form the First Patrol Boat Squadron, whose primary role is to support the University Royal Naval Units (URNU) but also contribute to a wide range of Fleet tasking. Commodore Britannia Royal Naval College has overall responsibility for the URNUs whose role is to educate and inform a wide spectrum of high calibre undergraduates. Vessels are assigned to the following URNUs: ARCHER (East Scotland); BITER (Manchester & Salford); BLAZER (Southampton); CHARGER (Liverpool); DASHER (Bristol); EXAMPLE (Northumbria); EXPLOIT (Birmingham); EXPLORER (Yorkshire); EXPRESS (Wales); PUNCHER (London); PURSUER (Glasgow & Strathclyde); RANGER (Sussex); SMITER (Oxford); TRUMPETER (Cambridge).

The last two vessels built, RAIDER and TRACKER, have a higher top speed of 24 knots as they are fitted with two MTU V12 diesels. They now comprise the Faslane Patrol Boat Squadron. Formed in March 2010, the Squadron provides Force Protection in and around Faslane, Scotland. Initially PURSUER and DASHER were relocated to HMNB Clyde from Cyprus in April 2010, arriving at their new home on 6 May that year. They were replaced by RAIDER and TRACKER in September 2012. They are fully-fledged armed patrol boats. Fitted with Kevlar armour and able to mount three 7.62mm General Purpose Machine Guns (GPMG) they are part of a growing Force Protection cadre based at Faslane to protect the UKs nuclear deterrent. These two vessels are fully engaged in FP duties and do not undertake university training.

The P2000s engines are being replaced by two CAT C18 Acert units to help reduce emissions, lower fuel consumption and improve efficiency. BITER was the first to be fitted during an extended refit, to be followed by EXPLORER, RANGER and EXPRESS. The programme, which will cover the entire 16- strong class will extend their lives by 15 years.

HMS Scott

SURVEY SHIPS
SCOTT CLASS

Ship	Pennant Number	Completion Date	Builder
SCOTT	H131	1997	Appledore

Displacement 13,300 tonnes **Dimensions** 131.5m x 21.5m x 9m **Speed** 17 knots **Complement** 63 (42 embarked at any one time)

Notes

Designed to commercial standards SCOTT provides the RN with a deep bathymetric capability off the continental shelf. Fitted with a modern multi-beam sonar suite she can conduct mapping of the ocean floor worldwide. She carries a mixture of the latest UK and US survey equipment. She operates a three watch system whereby the vessel is run by 42 of her ship's company of 63 - with the remainder on leave. Each crew member works 75 days in the ship before having 30 days ashore for leave, training and other duties, allowing her to spend more than 300 days at sea in a year. Extensive use of commercial lean manning methods including unmanned machinery spaces, fixed fire fighting systems and extensive machinery and safety surveillance technology. Her hull is Ice class 1A: Ships with such structure, engine output and other properties are capable of navigating in difficult ice conditions, but only with the assistance of icebreakers. In 2013 Babcock won a five year contract from the MoD to provide through life engineering support to the ship. In 2015 SCOTT emerged from an upgrade period at Devonport, during which she received a number of upgrades and improvements, including a new sewage treatment plant and new lifeboat davits, as well as a new uninterrupted power supply to the ship's sonar suite. She returned to sea for trials and training in May 2015.

HMS Echo

ECHO CLASS

Ship	Pennant Number	Completion Date	Builder
ECHO	H87	2002	Appledore
ENTERPRISE	H88	2003	Appledore

Displacement 3,500 tonnes **Dimensions** 90m x 16.8m x 5.5.m **Speed** 15 knots **Armament** 2 x 20mm **Complement** 49 (with accommodation for 81)

Notes

In June 2000, a £130 million order was placed with prime contractor Vosper Thornycroft to build and maintain, over a 25 year period, these two new Survey Vessels Hydrographic Oceanographic (SVHO). Both vessels were built by sub-contractor Appledore Shipbuilding Limited. They have a secondary role as mine countermeasures HQ ships. The total ship's company is 72, with 48 personnel onboard at any one time working a cycle of 75 days on, 30 days off, allowing the ships to be operationally available for 330 days a year. Utilizing a diesel electric propulsion system, they have three main generators. They are the first RN ships to be fitted with Azimuth pod thrusters in place of the more normal shaft and propellor. Each ship carries a named survey launch, SAPPHIRE (ECHO) and SPITFIRE (ENTERPRISE). SPITFIRE is a new design 9m SMB powered by two 6-cylinder diesels linked to jet propulsion units. It is equipped with side scan sonar and both multi-beam and single beam echo sounders. In June 2015 ENTERPRISE replaced BULWARK in support of the EU mission to tackle the migration crisis in the Mediterranean. By the end of October the ship had rescued 439 migrants.

HMS Gleaner

INSHORE SURVEY VESSEL

Ship	Pennant Number	Completion Date	Builder
GLEANER	H86	1983	Emsworth

Displacement 26 tons **Dimensions** 14.8m x 4.7m x 1.6m **Speed** 14 knots
Complement 8

Notes

Small inshore survey craft used for the collection of data from the shallowest inshore waters. She uses multi-beam and sidescan sonar to collect bathymetry and seabed texture data and compile an accurate and detailed picture of the seabed. She was scheduled to decommission in 2007, but she emerged, in 2008, from a Service Life Extension Programme, which will enable her to remain in service for a further 10 years. She carries the prefix Her Majesty's Survey Motor Launch or HMSML.

Four small survey boats, NESBITT, PAT BARTON, COOK and OWEN are attached to the Hydrographic School at Devonport.

HMS Protector

ICE PATROL SHIPS
PROTECTOR

Ship	Pennant Number	Completion Date	Builder
PROTECTOR	A173	2001	Havyard Leirvik (Norway)

Displacement 4,985 tons **Dimensions** 89.7m x 18m x 7.25m **Speed** 15 knots **Armament** Miniguns; GPMGs **Complement** 88

Notes

The ice-breaker MV POLARBJORN was initially leased, in June 2011, on a three-year contract from the Norwegian company GC Rieber Shipping as a temporary replacement for the damaged ENDURANCE and commissioned as PROTECTOR. In 2013 it was announced that the ship had been purchased by the MoD.

Although the ship has a flight deck, there is no hangar, so she will be unable to deploy with an embarked helicopter. However, for her latest deployment the ship has been given three 3D-printed micro-aircraft, identical to one tested on board HMS MERSEY in 2015 off the Dorset coast. The aircraft are controlled from a laptop on board, can cruise at nearly 60mph and are all but noiseless thanks to their tiny engine. Each one costs no more

than £7,000 – cheaper than an hour's flying time by a Fleet Air Arm helicopter. Each micro-aircraft can fly for up to 30 minutes, recording video footage on a miniscule camera, before setting down in the icy waters or on the snow and ice where it will be picked up by PROTECTOR's ship's company.
She also operates the Survey Motor Boat JAMES CAIRD IV and the 8.5 metre Rigid Work Boat TERRA NOVA. She can also deploy two Pacific 22 RIBs (NIMROD and AURORA). She also deploys with three BV206 all terrain vehicles and four quad bikes and trailers to assist in moving stores and equipment. In 2015, the ship changed her base port from Portsmouth, to join the rest of the Hydrographic Squadron at Devonport.

The ship sailed for her latest deployment in October 2015, but rather than operating in her more traditional waters of the South Atlantic, the ship headed east, visiting the Seychelles and Australia before embarking on survey operations in the Ross Sea, which has not been visited by a Royal Navy vessel for 80 years. The ship has eight different 'work packages' planned in and around Antarctica. Those spells of intensive work, making use of the warmer temperatures and less inclement weather of the Austral summer, will focus on updating charts of the waters for the UK Hydrographic Office, monitoring wildlife and assisting the work of international inspectors who visit the numerous scientific bases peppered around the Antarctic.

The ship is scheduled to be away from the UK until the spring of 2017. One third of her crew rotates every few weeks to sustain the ship on operations.

Her predecessor, ENDURANCE, which was decommissioned in 2012 following a flooding incident in 2008 has now been put up for sale. The Disposal Sales Agency (DSA) invited expressions of interest in July 2015 from interested parties. It was noted that following the 2008 incident the ship suffered catastrophic flooding from bilge to C deck across midships watertight section. Associated machinery, systems and accommodation were destroyed or badly damaged. No repair work has taken place. It is likely that the ship will be sold for recycling.

ROYAL MARINE CRAFT

RM Tamar, a newly built facility, housed at Devonport Naval Base, is home to the RMs Landing Craft, Hovercraft and other vessels when not required for deployment, either onboard the assault ships, or independently.

Based at RM Tamar is 1 Assault Group Royal Marines (1 AGRM), the lead for amphibious warfare and Royal Navy board and search training. The group is tasked with training and developing core amphibious and surface assault skills and equipment, including the provision of operational support for the Ministry of Defence.

1 AGRM is responsible for 4 subordinate units which deliver the vast spectrum of training and operations required in delivering amphibious and surface assault capability of the Royal Navy and Royal Marines.

10 (Landing Craft) Training Squadron - Responsible for delivering landing craftsmen training as well as small boats, engineering and assault navigation training.

11 Amphibious Trials and Training Squadron (Instow, North Devon) - Delivering training that covers the area between the craft and the beachhead. The Instow squadron also conducts the trials and testing of future craft.

The Royal Navy School of Board and Search at HMS Raleigh in Torpoint trains both individuals and ship's boarding teams to conduct the full range of boarding operations that is required by the Naval Service.

In addition, 1AGRM is also tasked with parenting the Assault Squadrons of the Royal Marines (ASRMs) and their Landing Craft detachments which are assigned to the amphibious assault ships. These ASRMs provide the landing craft and therefore the fighting capability for the RN's Amphibious Ships, OCEAN (9 ASRM); ALBION (6 ASRM - currently disbanded and operated as 6 Ops Sqn until ALBION returns to service) and BULWARK (4 ASRM).

43 Commando Fleet Protection Group Royal Marines (43 Cdo FP Gp RM) is based at HM Naval Base Clyde near Helensburgh on the West Coast of Scotland. Formerly Comacchio Group it was renamed in April 2012 and, together with 539 ASRM, became part of 3 Commando Brigade. The Group's core task is to provide military support to undertake final denial of access to nuclear weapons in addition to supporting the multi-agency force that protects nuclear weapons convoys. Additionally, specially trained teams are deployed at short notice to conduct tasks in support of the RN worldwide. Tasks have ranged from Force Protection, to conducting non-compliant boarding operations and counter-piracy operations.

Mull

ISLAND CLASS PATROL VESSELS

Ship	Pennant Number	Launch Date	Builder
RONA	-	2009	Holyhead Marine
MULL	-	2010	Holyhead Marine

Displacement 19.9 tonnes **Dimensions** 14.9m x 4.1m x 0.9m **Speed** 33 knots
Armament 4 x GPMG **Complement** 4

Notes

Originally units of a class of five launches delivered to the Ministry of Defence Police, RONA and MULL were transferred to 43 Commando Fleet Protection Group Royal Marines for operation on the Clyde to escort high value units. The vessels were returned to Holyhead Marine where they were modified in December 2012 and January 2013 respectively. As well as major reworking of their upper decks, the vessels were fitted with three new weapon mounts, enhanced protection for coxswains and crew, as well as an enhanced communications package.

LCU Mk10 B2

LCU Mk10

Ship	Pennant Number	Parent Unit	Builder
9730	P1	10 Trg Sqn, TAMAR	Ailsa, Troon
9731	P2	11 ATT Sqn, INSTOW	Ailsa, Troon
9732	A1	6 Ops Sqn, TAMAR	BAE Systems
9733	B2	HMS BULWARK	BAE Systems
9734	A2	10 Trg Sqn, TAMAR	BAE Systems
9735	B3	HMS BULWARK	BAE Systems
9736	A4	HMS BULWARK	BAE Systems
9737	B1	HMS BULWARK	BAE Systems
9738	B3	6 Ops Sqn, TAMAR	BAE Systems
9739	FJ	10 Trg Sqn, TAMAR	BAE Systems

Displacement 240 tonnes **Dimensions** 29.82m x 7.7m x 1.70m **Speed** 8.5 knots **Armament** 2 x GPMG **Complement** 7

34

Notes

Ro-Ro style landing craft designed to operate from the Albion class LPDs or Landing Ship Dock Auxiliary (LSD(A)). Ordered in 1998 from Ailsa Troon. The first two were delivered in 1999 with the final vessels being accepted into service in 2003. The remainder were built by BAE Systems at Govan. Capable of lifting one Main Battle Tank or four lighter vehicles. Capacity for 100 fully equipped troops. With a range of around 600 nautical miles – more if auxiliary tanks are added – they are designed to operate independently for 14 days with a seven man Royal Marine crew in both arctic and tropical climates. All the crew members have bunk accommodation and there is a galley and store rooms. Unlike other vessels, pennant numbers and parent units can change as the vessels are rotated through maintenance cycles.

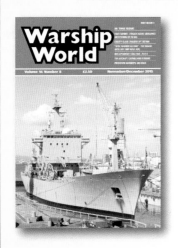

LCVP Mk5A/5B

Ship	Pennant Number	Parent Unit	Builder
Mk5A			
9707	-	10 Trg Sqn, TAMAR	Babcock Marine
9675	-	10 Trg Sqn, TAMAR	Vosper T.
9676	-	10 Trg Sqn, TAMAR	Vosper T.
Mk5B			
0202	A8	539 ASRM, TAMAR	Babcock Marine
0203	A6	HMS OCEAN	Babcock Marine
0204	A7	539 ASRM, TAMAR	Babcock Marine
0205	A5	10 Trg Sqn, TAMAR	Babcock Marine
0338	T6	11 ATT Sqn, INSTOW	Babcock Marine

Ship	Pennant Number	Parent Unit	Builder
0339	P6	10 Trg Sqn, TAMAR	Babcock Marine
0340	P7	HMS OCEAN	Babcock Marine
0341	P4	10 Trg Sqn, TAMAR	Babcock Marine
0344	NM	HMS BULWARK	Babcock Marine
0345	N2	HMS BULWARK	Babcock Marine
0346	N3	HMS OCEAN	Babcock Marine
0347	N4	HMS OCEAN	Babcock Marine
0353	B6	539 ASRM, TAMAR	Babcock Marine
0354		539 ASRM, TAMAR	Babcock Marine
0355	B7	HMS BULWARK	Babcock Marine
0356	B8	HMS BULWARK	Babcock Marine

Displacement 24 tonnes **Dimensions** 15.70m x 3.5m x 0.90m **Speed** 25 knots **Armament** 2 x GPMG **Complement** 3

Notes

First one ordered in 1995 from Vosper Thornycroft and handed over in 1996. A further four were delivered in December 1996 to operate from OCEAN, with two more for training at RM Poole ordered in 1998. A further 16 were ordered from Babcock in 2001 with the final vessels being accepted into service in 2004. The Mk 5 can lift 8 tonnes of stores or a mix of 2 tonnes and 35 troops. These vessels have a greater range, lift and speed than the Mk4s which they replaced. The primary role is the landing of vehicles, personnel and equipment onto potentially hostile shores. The secondary role is a general purpose support craft both between ships and ship to shore. The craft are capable of performing normal duties in conditions up to sea state 4 and run for cover up to sea state 5. Pennant numbers and parent units can change as the vessels are rotated through maintenance cycles.

Griffon 2400TD

4 GRIFFON 2400TD LCAC

Ship	Pennant Number	Completion Date	Builder
C21	-	2010	Griffon
C22	-	2010	Griffon
C23	-	2010	Griffon
C24	-	2010	Griffon

G.R.T. 6.8 tons **Dimensions** 13.4m x 6.8m **Speed** 45 knots **Range** 300 nm **Armament** 1 x GPMG **Complement** 2 Crew; 16 fully-equipped marines.

Notes

Operated by 539 Assault Squadron, the 2400TD offers greater payload, performance and obstacle clearance than the earlier 2000 TD craft. Centre sections of the cabin roof can be removed in order to embark two one-tonne NATO pallets. They can be transported on a standard low loader truck or in the hold of a C-130 Hercules aircraft. They can also operate directly from the well-deck of RN amphibious ships. They are equipped with a 7.62mm General Purpose Machine Gun, HF and VHF radios, radar, GPS, ballistic protection and a variety of specialised equipment. All four entered service by the end of 2010.

OFFSHORE RAIDING CRAFT

The Royal Marines operate two versions of the Offshore Raiding Craft (ORC), the Troop Carrying Variant (TCV) and Fire Support Variant (FSV). The ORC is an air portable surface manoeuvre craft designed for the rapid deployment of 8 fully equipped troops and 2 crew from over the horizon (30 miles) ship to shore and vice versa. They provide rapid movement of troops in coastal, estuarine, riverine and inland waters. Specifications: Weight: 3.6 tonnes - Length: 9.1m - Speed: 36 kts - Capacity: 2 Crew + 8 fully equipped troops.

RIGID RAIDING CRAFT

The Royal Marines operate a number of smaller Rigid-hulled and Rigid-Inflatable craft for various assault, patrol and security duties. There are 5.2, 6.5 and 8 metre long versions. Rigid Raiders feature GRP (glass reinforced plastic) hulls and early variants featured single or twin outboard motors. The latest RRC, the Mk3, is powered by an inboard diesel engine. They can carry up to eight troops.

SPECIALIST CRAFT

In addition to the familiar Rigid Raiding Craft and Rigid Inflatable Boats other specialist vessels are available including air transportable Fast Insertion Craft (FIC) with a speed of 55 knots in addition to advanced wave piercing designs. Swimmer Delivery Vehicles (SDV), in reality miniature submarines, which can be deployed from dry deck shelters on larger submarines, are also operated as a part of the UK Special Forces inventory.

Following trials with Swedish CP90 Combat Boats, the Royal Marines were hopeful of procuring a new Force Protection Craft, based on experience with the CB 90s, capable of landing troops and protecting the landing craft from seaborne and land based threats. An in service date of 2016 was anticipated, but to date there has been little indication of progress with this programme.

SHIPS FOR THE FUTURE FLEET

JOHN NEWTH

QUEEN ELIZABETH CLASS AIRCRAFT CARRIERS

After a decade of design studies, a contract for the construction of two aircraft carriers, QUEEN ELIZABETH and PRINCE OF WALES, the largest warships to be designed and built in the UK, was signed in July 2008 between the Government and the Aircraft Carrier Alliance, an industrial group comprising BAE Systems Surface Ships, Babcock Marine, Thales and the Ministry of Defence.

The ships are being built in sections constructed by BAE Systems at Govan, Scotstoun and Portsmouth; Babcock in Rosyth and Appledore; Cammell Laird in Birkenhead and A & P, Tyne and are being assembled in Number 1 Dock at Rosyth. The dock at Rosyth has had the entrance widened from 124 feet to 138 feet. The sides were re-profiled with the removal of angled steps to make the dock floor 30 feet wider. A new overhead crane with a span of 394 feet, named Goliath, has been installed to straddle the dock and lift the smaller blocks into place. The individual blocks are built under cover and fitted out with machinery and sub-assemblies such as diesel generators, offices, cabins and galleys before they are moved to Rosyth.

The completed ships will be 284 metres long with a waterline beam of 39 metres and beam across the flight deck of 73 metres. Height from the bottom of the hull to the masthead will be 57.5 metres and draught 11 metres. There are 9 decks in the hull with another 9 in the two islands. Each ship is expected to be in the dock for two years and will be 'floated out' into the adjacent non-tidal basin for completion.

The 2010 SDSR determined that the new carriers should operate the conventional F-35C 'tail-hook' variant of the Joint Strike fighter, rather than the intended F-35B STOVL variant and be converted for 'cat & trap' operations. The Conversion Development Phase was scheduled to run to late 2012. However, concerns as to the affordability of the CV conversion prompted the MoD to reconsider the STOVL option in an attempt to finalise its PR12 budget planning round and balance the equipment programme.

According to the MoD, work undertaken had revealed that the CV-capable carrier strike capability would not be ready until 2023, some three years later than originally planned. Furthermore, the cost of fitting the Electromagnetic Aircraft Launch System (EMALS), Advanced Arresting Gear (AAG) and other CV aviation systems into PRINCE OF WALES was now estimated at £2 billion, over double the initial estimate of £950 million.

In his statement to parliament, the Secretary of State for Defence said that the SDSR decision on carriers "was right at the time, but the facts have changed and therefore so too must our approach".

He added: "Carrier strike with 'cats and traps' using the Carrier Variant jet no longer represents the best way of delivering carrier strike and I am not prepared to tolerate a three year further delay to reintroducing our Carrier Strike capability." The MoD initially said that about £40 million had been spent to date on the Carrier Conversion Development Phase. However, he later admitted that the total cost of the u-turn, taking into account other costs and penalties, came to about £100 million.

Her Majesty Queen Elizabeth II formally named the future HMS QUEEN ELIZABETH at Babcock's Rosyth dockyard on 4 July 2014. A little less than a fortnight later, on 17 July, the ship was floated out of No.1 dock at Rosyth dockyard in Fife to an outfitting berth in the adjacent basin. Fitting out continues ahead of sea trials beginning in August 2016 and delivery in May 2017. Helicopter flying trials are scheduled for 2017 and fixed wing trials with the F-35B towards the end of 2018. An operational military capability will be declared in 2020.

On 9 September, Lower Block 03 (LB03) and Lower Block 02 (LB02) of PRINCE OF WALES were docked down into the build dock at Rosyth, marking the start of the assembly phase for PRINCE OF WALES. In October 2015 26,500t of the forward half of the ship was mechanically skidded back in the dry dock to the 12,000t superblock which makes up the rear of the vessel. Construction of the second ship is proceeding at a greater pace than the first. Construction of the 300m-long and 74m-wide vessel is scheduled for completion in July 2016. Following fitting out the ship is scheduled to begin sea trials in January 2019, followed by acceptance in August of the same year.

TYPE 26 FRIGATE (GLOBAL COMBAT SHIP)

Conceived as a multi-mission warship designed for joint and multi-national operations across the full spectrum of warfare, the Type 26 is planned to progressively replace the Type 23 frigates from the early part of the next decade.

The ships will employ a Combined Diesel Electric or Gas Turbine propulsion system. This will enable the ships to achieve high speeds, whilst also providing an economic power to the onboard systems and will allow the ships to operate quietly in cruising mode. Rolls-Royce has been selected as the design partner for Gas Turbines, while David Brown Gear Systems Ltd will develop the Gear box and MTU the Diesel Generator Sets. Rohde & Schwarz has been selected to design the Integrated Communications System for the ships. In September 2015 it was announced that BAE will provide the Integrated Gunnery System for the ships, the gun chosen being the Mk 45 Mod 4 5-in/62 calibre gun. The deal also includes an automated ammunition handling system and a fire control system. It is also likely that the Lockheed Martin Mk 41 VLS system will be selected to meet the requirement for a 24-cell Flexible Strike Silo. The ship will be able to support Wildcat or Merlin helicopters as well as having a flightdeck capable of landing a Chinook with the ramp down to embark troops. Forward of the hangar will be a mission bay enabling the ship to carry differing payloads depending on operational requirements.

The Assessment Phase for the Type 26 programme began in March 2010, with a Main Investment decision by the end of 2014, but this was delayed until after the Scottish independence referendum. In February 2015, the MoD and BAE Systems signed a contract worth £859m to continue development, supporting progression towards the manufacturing phase, which is scheduled to start in 2016; the first vessel is due to enter service in the early 2020s. Current plans call for a class of 13 ships to replace the current Type 23s on a one-for-one basis but there has also been mention of a class of "up to" 13 ships.

BATCH 2 RIVER CLASS

Steel was cut, on 10 October 2014, for the first of three new Batch 2 River class offshore patrol vessels, HMS FORTH, at a ceremony in Glasgow with construction of the third of the trio, HMS TRENT, beginning in October 2015. The plan to build three OPVs was announced in November 2013 and a manufacturing contract was placed with BAE Systems in August 2014.

The ships, based on the 90m vessels in service with Brazil and Thailand, have been ordered as part of a deal to sustain key industrial capabilities between the completion of the Queen Elizabeth-class carriers and the start of the Type 26 programme. At £348 million (compared to £150 million for the three Brazilian Amazonas class) these are very expensive vessels - being built to keep a shipyard in work rather than for any operational imperative.

The basic design has been modified to meet specific RN requirements including a strengthened flight deck to operate a Merlin helicopter; modified and uprated helicopter in-flight refuelling arrangements; additional accommodation for embarked military detachments and improved watertight integrity and firefighting equipment. At 2,000-tonnes the ship will have a range of 5,000 miles and could be deployed in support of UK interests both at home and abroad. The ships will be armed with a single MSI-Defence Systems 30mm gun and two Mk 44 mini-guns. They will also be fitted with a variant of BAE's CMS-1 combat management system and a SCANTER 4103 I-band radar.

HMS FORTH is expected to begin sea trials in 2016 and be handed over in spring 2017. The second, to be named MEDWAY, will be delivered in October 2017 and the third, to be named TRENT, in July 2018.

The future RFA TIDESPRING fitting out at DSME Shipyard, South Korea

MILITARY AFLOAT REACH AND SUSTAINABILITY (MARS)

The future re-equipment of the RFA rests with this programme in which it is envisioned 11 ships will be procured (five fleet tankers - delivered 2011 to 2015; three joint sea-based logistics vessels - 2016, 2017 and 2020; Two fleet solid-support ships - 2017 and 2020 and a single fleet tanker - 2021).

At the end of 2007 the MoD invited industry to express their interest in the project to build up to six fleet tankers. In May 2008 four companies had been shortlisted to submit proposals for the design and construction of the ships however, this project was deferred in December 2008, the MoD announcing that having reviewed all the components of the MARS fleet auxiliary programme it was concluded that there was scope for considering alternative approaches to its procurement. Post SDSR the government stated that the requirement for the MARS programme is driven by the logistic support needs of the future RN; these being assessed following the outcome of the SDSR. It now seems likely that MARS will deliver just seven vessels (four tankers and up to three solid-support ships).

In February 2012 the MoD announced that Daewoo Shipbuilding and Marine Engineering (DSME) of South Korea were the preferred bidder in a £425 million contract to build four 37,000 tonne tankers for the RFA, the first of which is planned to enter service in 2016. They will form a new Tide class, being named TIDESPRING, TIDERACE, TIDESURGE and TIDEFORCE.

The principal particulars of the design include an overall length of 200.9 metres, a breadth of 28.6 metres, a draught of 10 metres, and a displacement (full load) of just

45

over 37,000 tonnes. Replenishment facilities comprise: three abeam RAS(L) stations (two sited starboard and one to port) for diesel oil, aviation fuel and fresh water; solid RAS reception up to 2 tonnes; and vertical replenishment using an embarked helicopter (the design features a flight deck sized for a Merlin, a maintenance hangar, and an in-flight refuelling capability). Provision is also made for the future fit of a stern fuel delivery reel.

In March 2015 it was announced that A&P Group, the UK's largest ship repair and conversion business, had been awarded a multi-million pound MoD contract to fit-out the tankers with their sensitive military equipment, work that will be undertaken at their Falmouth facility.

The building of the first vessel, TIDESPRING, began in South Korea in June 2014, with the building of each vessel scheduled to take 10 months. She is scheduled to be delivered to the MoD in December 2015 for final fitting out, followed by the others at six monthly intervals - the final delivery being planned for 15 April 2017. The A&P Group will provide through-life support to all four ships for a minimum of three years. The working life expectancy of the ships is 25 years.

With the tanker programme now under contract, the MoD is turning its attention towards the other MARS component in the shape of the Future Solid Support (FSS) programme. This second element of the modernisation of the RFA is intended to introduce replacements for RFAs FORT AUSTIN, FORT ROSALIE and FORT VICTORIA from the early 2020s.

The FSS design will deliver bulk ammunition, dry stores and food to support both carrier strike and littoral manoeuvre operations. Current plans assume a total of three FSS vessels, each displacing approximately 40,000 tonnes.

SUCCESSOR SUBMARINE PROGRAMME

The Successor programme envisages the delivery of three or four SSBNs to replace the RN's four existing Vanguard-class submarines from 2028 to maintain Continuous Att-Sea Deterrence (CASD). Initial gate approval was announced by the MoD in May 2011, marking the transition from the programme's concept phase to the current assessment phase. Assessment phase activities will finalise the Successor design, fund long lead items and start industrialisation to support manufacture. However, the key main gate investment decision - which will commit to construction and also determine whether CASD can be delivered by three or four boats - will not be taken until 2016, which is when the Government will decide whether or not to approve full production.

Work on the concept design phase for a submarine to replace the Vanguard class has been ongoing since 2007 and an outline submarine design has been selected. Work with the US on a Common Missile Compartment is ongoing to evaluate how best to incorporate the UK's requirement for eight operational missiles, against a baseline design for the CMC which currently involves a 12 missile tube unit. It has been recognised that the cost of the CMC will be minimised by keeping as much of the design as possible in common with the US.

In 2012 two contracts worth £350 million each were awarded by the MoD to enable detailed design work to continue on both the submarine design and the new PWR3 nuclear reactor. In March 2015 BAE Systems was awarded additional funding of £257M to cover the final phase of work. The programme recently passed a major design review and is now more than halfway through its five-year Assessment Phase. Although a decision on the final design and build will not be made until 2016, detailed work has to take place now to ensure that the Successor submarines can begin to be delivered in 2028.

THE ROYAL FLEET AUXILIARY

The Royal Fleet Auxiliary (RFA) is a civilian manned fleet, owned by the Ministry of Defence. Traditionally, its main task has been to replenish warships of the Royal Navy at sea with fuel, food, stores and ammunition to extend their operations away from base support. However, as the RN surface fleet has shrunk, the RFA has shrunk with it but it has also acted as a 'force multiplier' being able to take on some operational roles. By embarking helicopters, tankers and stores ships have been deployed on RN patrol tasks in the Caribbean and on counter-piracy operations. By embarking ASW helicopters they are also able to provide additional warfare support to task group operations. Like the RN, the RFA are suffering manpower shortages, particularly in the engineering specialisation, and it has been noticeable that at least three ships have spent extended periods alongside in 2015, reportedly laid-up due to lack of engineering staff, although the MoD are keen to confirm that those ships remain in the operational cycle.

Legislation banning the use of single-hulled tankers in 2010 is driving the need for replacement ships. There are three such dedicated tankers in-service with the RFA with a further general replenishment ship that has a tanking capability. However, such is the delay in the new tanker programme that the two Rover class tankers have had their service lives extended by a further seven years - making them 42 years old before they are expected to finally pay off. RFA GOLD ROVER commenced her final operational deployment in 2014 and is expected to be replaced by the first of the Tide class on her return.

As part of the Military Afloat Reach and Sustainability (MARS) programme, the MoD placed an order in 2012 for four tankers to be built in South Korea. They will be named TIDESPRING, TIDERACE, TIDESURGE and TIDEFORCE with the first of class entering service in 2016 (see page 45).

The long term maintenance of the RFA fleet rests with shipyards in the North West, North East and South West of England. Cammell Laird Shiprepairers & Shipbuilders Ltd of Birkenhead and the A&P Group in Falmouth and Newcastle-upon-Tyne were named as the contractors to maintain the flotilla of 16 RFA tankers, stores and landing ships. They maintain 'clusters' of ships, providing the necessary refuelling and refit work for the RFA vessels throughout their service lives. Ships are grouped in clusters according to their duties and capabilities. A&P Group are charged with two clusters (Cluster 1: ARGUS and Cluster 2: CARDIGAN BAY, LYME BAY, MOUNTS BAY) in a contract worth around £53 million with the work to be shared between its bases in Falmouth and on the Tyne, while CL Ltd is contracted for the maintenance of four clusters of ships (Cluster 3: BLACK ROVER, GOLD ROVER; Cluster 4: DILIGENCE, WAVE KNIGHT, WAVE RULER; Cluster 5: FORT AUSTIN, FORT ROSALIE and Cluster 6: FORT VICTORIA).

SHIPS OF THE ROYAL FLEET AUXILIARY
Pennant Numbers

Ship	Pennant Number	Page	Ship	Pennant Number	Page
Tankers			**Amphibious Ships**		
GOLD ROVER	A271	51	LYME BAY	L3007	54
BLACK ROVER	A273	51	MOUNTS BAY	L3008	54
WAVE KNIGHT	A389	50	CARDIGAN BAY	L3009	54
WAVE RULER	A390	50			
			Repair Ship		
Stores Ships					
			DILIGENCE	A132	55
FORT ROSALIE	A385	52			
FORT AUSTIN	A386	52	**Primary Casualty Receiving Ship/Aviation Training Ship**		
Stores Ship/Tankers					
			ARGUS	A135	56
FORT VICTORIA	A387	53			

FAST FLEET TANKERS
WAVE CLASS

Ship	Pennant Number	Completion Date	Builder
WAVE KNIGHT	A 389	2002	BAe Systems
WAVE RULER	A 390	2002	BAe Systems

Displacement 31,500 tons (Full Load) **Dimensions** 196 x 27 x 10m **Speed** 18 knots
Armament 2 x Vulcan Phalanx, 2 x 30mm **Aircraft** Up to 2 Merlin **Complement** 80
(plus 22 Fleet Air Arm)

Notes

These 31,500-tonne ships are diesel-electric powered, with three refuelling rigs. They have a cargo capacity of 16,900 tonnes (Fuel) and 915 tonnes (Dry Stores). They have a large one spot flight deck, hangar and maintenance facilities capable of supporting two Merlin helicopters. They have spent extended periods in the Caribbean conducting successful counter-narcotics operations with an embarked RN helicopter. WAVE RULER, which has been deployed as the Gulf Ready Tanker since August 2013 was relieved by FORT VICTORIA in July 2015.

RFA Black Rover

SMALL FLEET TANKERS

ROVER CLASS

Ship	Pennant Number	Completion Date	Builder
GOLD ROVER	A271	1974	Swan Hunter
BLACK ROVER	A273	1974	Swan Hunter

Displacement 11,522 tons **Dimensions** 141m x 19m x 7m **Speed** 18 knots **Armament** 2 - 20mm guns **Complement** 49/54

Notes

Small Fleet Tankers designed to supply warships with fresh water, dry cargo and refrigerated provisions, as well as a range of fuels and lubricants. Helicopter deck, but no hangar. Have been employed in recent years mainly as support for HM Ships operating around the Falkland Islands and as the FOST station tanker. Now over 40 years old, GOLD ROVER sailed to the South Atlantic for her final deployment in September 2014. On her return in 2016 she will be decommissioned. BLACK ROVER was scheduled to conduct a further deployment in 2016 prior to decommissioning in 2017, but she remains laid up at Birkenhead being destored prior to refit, but given current manpower issues it is unknown whether this will take place or if the vessel will return to service.

The last of the Bay class Support Tankers, ORANGELEAF, decommissioned at Birkenhead on 28 September 2015. The MoD also has the commercial tanker MAERSK RAPIER under charter which supplies fuel to the naval facilities in the UK and abroad. The MoD charters the vessel to commercial companies when it is not in use for their own requirements. The tanker MT CUMBRIAN FISHER has also been occasionally chartered for moving fuel products between the UK and the Falkland Islands.

RFA Fort Austin

STORES VESSELS
FORT CLASS I

Ship	Pennant Number	Completion Date	Builder
FORT ROSALIE	A385	1978	Scott Lithgow
FORT AUSTIN	A386	1979	Scott Lithgow

Displacement 23,384 tons **Dimensions** 183m x 24m x 9m **Armament** 2 x Vulcan Phalanx **Speed** 20 knots **Complement** 201, (120 RFA, 36 MoD Civilians & 45 Fleet Air Arm)

Notes

Full hangar and maintenance facilities are provided and up to four Sea King or Lynx helicopters can be carried for both the transfer of stores and anti-submarine protection of a group of ships (note: these ships are not cleared to operate Merlin). Both ships can be armed with 4 - 20mm guns. FORT AUSTIN received two Vulcan Phalanx mounts sited to port and starboard above the bridge wings. FORT AUSTIN arrived at Birkenhead in 2015 following her Gulf deployment where she remains laid up awaiting refit. Her sister FORT ROSALIE is working up having been at Birkenhead since January 2013. FORT AUSTIN is scheduled to decommission in 2021 and FORT ROSALIE in 2022.

RFA Fort Victoria

REPLENISHMENT SHIPS
FORT CLASS II

Ship	Pennant Number	Completion Date	Builder
FORT VICTORIA	A387	1992	Harland & Wolff

Displacement 35,500 tons **Dimensions** 204m x 30m x 9m **Speed** 20 knots **Armament** 4 - 30mm guns, 2 x Phalanx CIWS, Sea Wolf Missile System (Fitted for but not with) **Complement** 100 (RFA), 24 MoD Civilians, 32 RN and up to 122 Fleet Air Arm

Notes

A "One stop" replenishment ship with the widest range of armaments, fuel and spares carried. Can operate up to 5 Sea King/Lynx or 3 Merlin Helicopters (more in a ferry role) with full maintenance facilities onboard. Medical facilities were upgraded with a 12 bed surgical capability. Under current plans she is to remain in service until 2019. She returned to the UK on 9 December 2013 following a 1,197 day deployment to the Gulf. She completed a £50m refit in December 2014 and is now deployed in support of operations east of Suez, having relieved both WAVE RULER and FORT AUSTIN, where she will remain for several years.

RFA Lyme Bay

LANDING SHIP DOCK (AUXILIARY) BAY CLASS

Ship	Pennant Number	Completion Date	Builder
LYME BAY	L3007	2007	Swan Hunter
MOUNTS BAY	L3008	2006	BAe Systems
CARDIGAN BAY	L3009	2007	BAe Systems

Displacement 16,190 tonnes **Dimensions** 176.6m x 26.4m x 5.1m **Speed** 18 knots **Armament** 2 x Vulcan Phalanx in some **Complement** 60

Notes

The dock is capable of operating LCU 10s and they carry two LCVP Mk5s. They can offload at sea, over the horizon. In addition to their war fighting role they could be well suited to disaster relief and other humanitarian missions. Since 2010, vessels emerging from refit have received two funnels running up the side of the midships gantry. These were resited due to problems with fumes over the aft end of the flightdeck. Additional mini-gun emplacements have been added at the stern (in place of the aft funnels) and amidships. CARDIGAN BAY is deployed to the Gulf and is fitted with two Phalanx CIWS mounts to port and starboard. LYME BAY emerged from refit with Phalanx mounts sited forward of the superstructure and on top of the aft end of the superstructure. In 2015 she was deployed to the Caribbean where she provided humanitarian aid in the aftermath of several hurricanes which devastated communities on Dominica and islands in the Bahamas. MOUNTS BAY sailed for post refit sea v trials in October 2015 having been laid up at Falmouth since January 2014.

RFA Diligence

FORWARD REPAIR SHIP

Ship	Pennant Number	Completion Date	Builder
DILIGENCE	A132	1981	Oesundsvarvet

Displacement 10,595 tons **Dimensions** 120m x 12m x 3m **Speed** 15 knots **Armament** 2 - 20mm **Complement** RFA 40, RN Personnel - approx 100

Notes

Formerly the MV STENA INSPECTOR purchased (£25m) for service in the South Atlantic. Her deep diving complex was removed. She is fitted with a wide range of workshops for hull and machinery repairs, as well as facilities for supplying electricity, water, fuel, air, steam, cranes and stores to other ships and submarines. When not employed on battle repair duties she can serve as a support vessel for MCMVs and submarines on deployment. Deployed as part of the Response Force Task Group in 2013 she remained deployed east of Suez in support of National Tasking until returning to the UK in September 2014 to undertake a refit at Birkenhead but, to date, remains laid up. This very useful vessel is nearing the end of her operational life but there is no evidence of a replacement strategy.

RFA Argus

PRIMARY CASUALTY RECEIVING SHIP/AVIATION TRAINING SHIP

Ship	Pennant Number	Completion Date	Builder
ARGUS	A135	1981	Cantieri Navali Breda

Displacement 28,481 tons (full load) **Dimensions** 175m x 30m x 8m **Speed** 18 knots **Armament** 4 - 30 mm, 2 - 20 mm **Complement** 254 (inc 137 Fleet Air Arm) **Aircraft** 6 Sea King/Merlin.

Notes

The former MV CONTENDER BEZANT was purchased in 1984 and rebuilt at Harland and Wolff, Belfast, from 1984-87 to operate as an Aviation Training Ship. She undertook a rapid conversion in October 1990 to become a Primary Casualty Receiving Ship (PCRS) for service in the Gulf. These facilities were upgraded and made permanent during 2001. In 2009 the ship underwent a Service Life Extension Programme at Falmouth to switch her primary role to that of PCRS with a secondary aviation training role. The construction of new casualty access lifts together with a new deckhouse aft of the superstructure has reduced helicopter capability by one landing spot. The ship has facilities for undertaking 3 major operations simultaneously, intensive care, high dependency and general wards for up to 100 patients. It also has a dentistry operating theatre, CT scanner and X-ray units. The care facility operates with a staff of up to 250 doctors, nurses and support staff. The ship is scheduled to remain in service until 2020. In October 2014 she deployed off Sierra Leone for six months in support of military and foreign aid personnel ashore who were fighting the Ebola outbreak. She returned to the UK in April 2015 and has since been involved in flying training operations off the UK coast.

MV Anvil Point

STRATEGIC SEALIFT RO-RO VESSELS
POINT CLASS

Ship	Pennant Number	Completion Date	Builder
HURST POINT		2002	Flensburger
HARTLAND POINT		2002	Harland & Wolff
EDDYSTONE		2002	Flensburger
ANVIL POINT		2003	Harland & Wolff

Displacement 10,000 tonnes, 13,300 tonnes (FL) **Dimensions** 193m x 26m x 6.6m
Speed 18 knots **Complement** 38

Notes

Foreland Shipping Limited operated 6 Ro-Ro vessels built at yards in the UK and Germany under a PFI deal which was signed with the MoD on 27 June 2002 and runs until 31 December 2024. While the current main focus is on transporting equipment to and from the Middle East/Gulf in support of military activities in Afghanistan, the vessels also make regular voyages to the Falkland Islands and to Canada and Norway in support of training exercises. The ships are all named after English lighthouses. The ships come under the operational umbrella of Defence Supply Chain Operation and Movements (DSCOM), part of the Defence Logistics Organisation. In 2012 the requirement was reduced from six to four ships. BEACHY HEAD and LONGSTONE were subsequently sold. The former has been renamed WILLIAMSBORG and is operated under the Maltese flag. The latter has been operating a Ro-Ro service in Australian waters between Burnie and Melbourne. HARTLAND POINT was deployed with OCEAN and BULWARK as part of the Cougar 2015 task group.

HMS BULWARK

David Hannaford

BAE Systems

HMS ARTFUL

Andy Mahon

HMS MERSEY

HMS ECHO

Derek Fox

HMS LANCASTER

SD POWERFUL

SERCO MARINE SERVICES

The tugs DEPENDABLE, BOUNTIFUL, INDEPENDENT and INDULGENT deployed to Barrow in August 2015 to assist the submarine ARTFUL during her exit from the shipbuilders at the start of her sea trials. (BAE Systems)

In December 2007 the MoD signed a £1 billion Private Finance Initiative (PFI) contract with Serco Denholm Marine Services Limited for the Future Provision of Marine Services (FPMS) over the following 15 years. In 2009 Serco bought out Denholm's share and the SD funnel logos have been replaced by a prominent Serco logo on the superstructure.

Marine services embrace a wide range of waterborne and associated support activities, both in and out of port, at Portsmouth, Devonport and on the Clyde, as well as maintenance of UK and overseas moorings and navigational marks and support of a range of military operations and training.

In-port services include the provision of berthing and towage activities within the three naval bases; passenger transportation, including pilot transfers and the transportation of stores, including liquids and munitions. The recovery and disposal of waste from ships and spillage prevention and clean-up also fall within their tasking. There is also a requirement for substantial out-of-port operations. Diving training, minelaying exercises, torpedo recovery, boarding training and target towing duties are also undertaken.

The Briggs Group has been sub-contracted to assist with buoys and mooring support work. Shore based work to support these moorings and navigation buoys, have been relocated from Pembroke Dock to Burntisland on the Firth of Forth.

Initially all vessels were repainted with red funnels and black hulls, the white line having been removed as were, in most cases, the pennant numbers. All names are now prefixed with the letters 'SD' and all vessels fly the red ensign. In 2012, the last vestiges of the former Royal Maritime Auxiliary Service identity were removed as, gradually, the whole fleet adopts a new colour scheme with the buff superstructure being repainted white.

SHIPS OF
SERCO MARINE SERVICES

SD Impetus

TUGS

IMPULSE CLASS

Ship	Completion Date	Builder
SD IMPULSE	1993	R. Dunston
SD IMPETUS	1993	R. Dunston

G.R.T. 400 tons approx **Dimensions** 33m x 10m x 4m **Speed** 12 knots **Complement** 5

Notes

Completed in 1993 specifically to serve as berthing tugs for the Trident Class submarines at Faslane. To be retained in service until 2022.

SD Indulgent

ASD 2509 CLASS

Ship	Completion Date	Builder
SD INDEPENDENT	2009	Damen, Gorinchem
SD INDULGENT	2009	Damen, Gorinchem

G.R.T. 345 tons approx **Dimensions** 26.09m x 9.44m x 4.3m **Speed** 13 knots **Complement** 5

Notes

Azimuth Stern Drive (ASD) tugs. Designed for Coastal and Harbour towage, specifically modified for making cold moves within the Naval Bases. Both are based at Portsmouth.

SD Bountiful

ATD 2909 CLASS

Ship	Completion Date	Builder
SD RELIABLE	2009	Damen, Stellendam
SD BOUNTIFUL	2010	Damen, Stellendam
SD RESOURCEFUL	2010	Damen, Stellendam
SD DEPENDABLE	2010	Damen, Stellendam

G.R.T. 271 tons **Dimensions** 29.14m x 9.98m x 4.8m **Speed** 13.1 knots **Complement** 5 (Accommodation for 6)

Notes

Azimuthing Tractor Drive (ATD) tugs. SD BOUNTIFUL is based at Portsmouth. SD RESOURCEFUL, SD RELIABLE and SD DEPENDABLE are based on the Clyde. Designed for Coastal and Harbour towage, specifically modified for making cold moves within the Naval Bases. Two double drum towing winches are fitted, along with extensive underwater fendering, fire fighting equipment and facilities for passenger and stores transportation.

SD Faithful

TWIN UNIT TRACTOR TUGS

Ship	Completion Date	Builder
SD ADEPT	1980	R. Dunston
SD CAREFUL	1982	R. Dunston
SD FAITHFUL	1985	R. Dunston
SD FORCEFUL	1985	R. Dunston
SD POWERFUL	1985	R. Dunston

(A221)
(A223) —

G.R.T. 384 tons **Dimensions** 38.8m x 9.42m x 4m **Speed** 12 knots **Complement** 5

Notes

The principal harbour tugs in naval service. Some are to undergo a service life extension programme. All based at Devonport except SD POWERFUL, which is based at Portsmouth, but is sent to Devonport to cover Vanguard class movements if one of the other tugs is out of service.

69

SD Hercules

STAN TUG 2608 CLASS

Ship	Completion Date	Builder
SD HERCULES	2009	Damen, Gorinchem
SD JUPITER	2009	Damen, Gorinchem
SD MARS	2009	Damen, Gorinchem

G.R.T. 133.92 tons **Dimensions** 26.61m x 8.44m x 4.05m **Speed** 12 knots **Complement** 4 (6 max)

Notes

A conventional Twin Screw Tug design. SD HERCULES and SD MARS are based at Devonport. SD JUPITER is based on the Clyde. All can be used to handle submarine mounted Towed Arrays.

SD Suzanne

ASD 2009 CLASS

Ship	Completion Date	Builder
SD CHRISTINA	2010	Damen, Gdynia
SD DEBORAH	2010	Damen, Gdynia
SD EILEEN	2010	Damen, Gdynia
SD SUZANNE	2010	Damen, Gdynia

G.R.T. 120.74 tons **Dimensions** 21.2m x 9.4m x 3.6m **Speed** 11 knots **Complement** 3/4

Notes

Azimuth Stern Drive tugs derived from the successful Damen ASD 2411 shiphandling tug. Winches fore and aft, together with a bow thruster, make these tugs suitable for handling smaller surface ship, barge work and assisting with submarine movements. SD DEBORAH and SD EILEEN are based at Devonport, SD CHRISTINA and SD SUZANNE at Portsmouth.

SD Helen

FELICITY CLASS

Ship	Completion Date	Builder
SD FLORENCE	1980	R. Dunston
SD FRANCES	1980	R. Dunston
SD GENEVIEVE	1980	R. Dunston
SD HELEN	1974	R. Dunston

G.R.T. 88.96 tons **Dimensions** 22.0m x 6.4m x 2.6m **Speed** 10 knots **Complement** 4

Notes

Water Tractors used for the movement of small barges and equipment. SD FRANCES and SD FLORENCE based at Devonport, with the other pair at Portsmouth.

SD Catherine

PUSHY CAT 1204

Ship	Completion Date	Builder
SD CATHERINE	2008	Damen, Gorinchem
SD EMILY	2008	Damen, Gorinchem

G.R.T. 29.4 tons **Dimensions** 12.3m x 4.13m x 1.55m **Speed** 8 knots **Complement** 2

Notes

Powered by a single Caterpillar 3056 TA diesel driving a single screw. A propulsion nozzle is fitted, and twin rudders to give a 2.1 tons bollard pull. SD CATHERINE is based at Portsmouth, SD EMILY at Devonport. General line runner and harbour work-boat.

SD Tilly

STAN TUG 1405

Ship	Completion Date	Builder
SD TILLY	2009	Damen, Gorinchem

G.R.T. 45 tons **Dimensions** 14.55m x 4.98m x 1.8m **Speed** 9 knots **Complement** 3

Notes

A general purpose inshore and harbour tug based at Devonport. A twin screw version of the Pushy Cat 1204. Slightly larger with a bow thruster and also developing 8 tonnes bollard pull. Line handler, general workboat and ideal for moving small barges.

• DEREK FOX

SD Victoria

WORLDWIDE SUPPORT VESSEL

Ship	Completion Date	Builder
SD VICTORIA	2010	Damen, Galatz

G.R.T. 3,522 tons **Dimensions** 83m x 16m x 4.5m **Speed** 14 knots **Complement** 16 (Accommodation for 72)

Notes

Powered by two Caterpillar 3516B diesels driving two shafts with controllable pitch propellers SD VICTORIA is designed to support training operations around the world. Capable of transporting both personnel and equipment and supporting diving operations. She is equipped with classrooms, briefing rooms and operations rooms in addition to workshop facilities. There is provision to carry and operate RIBs and there is a helicopter winching deck. Note Fast Interceptor Craft under covers on the quarterdeck. Based at Greenock but spends time in Devonport loading for her various customers.

SD Warden

TRIALS VESSEL

Ship	Completion Date	Builder
SD WARDEN	1989	Richards

Displacement 626 tons **Dimensions** 48m x 10m x 4m **Speed** 15 knots **Complement** 11

Notes

Built as a Range Maintenance Vessel but now based at Kyle of Lochalsh and operated in support of BUTEC. Also operates as a Remotely Operated Vehicle (ROV) platform. A replacement ROV has been installed and set to work to replace the older system. To remain in service until 2022.

SD Kyle of Lochalsh

TRIALS VESSEL

Ship	Completion Date	Builder
SD KYLE OF LOCHALSH	1997	Abel, Bristol

Displacement 120 tons **Dimensions** 24.35m x 9m x 3.45m **Speed** 10.5 knots **Complement** 4

Notes

The former twin screw tug MCS LENIE which has now been purchased from Maritime Craft Services (Clyde) Ltd by Serco Marine Services. The 24.35m tug, built in 1997 by Abel in Bristol, is powered by Caterpillar main engines producing a total of 2,200bhp for a bollard pull of 26 tons. She is used to support trials and operations at Kyle of Lochalsh.

SD Cawsand

TENDERS
STORM CLASS

Ship	Completion Date	Builder
SD BOVISAND	1997	FBM (Cowes)
SD CAWSAND	1997	FBM (Cowes)

G.R.T 225 tonnes **Dimensions** 23m x 11m x 2m **Speed** 15 knots **Complement** 5

Notes

These craft are used in support of Flag Officer Sea Training (FOST) at Plymouth to transfer staff quickly and comfortably to and from Warships and Auxiliaries within and beyond the Plymouth breakwater in open sea conditions. These are the first vessels of a small waterplane area twin hull (SWATH) design to be ordered by the Ministry of Defence and cost £6.5 million each. Speed restrictions implemented due to wash problems generated by these vessels. To remain in service until 2022.

SD Netley

NEWHAVEN CLASS

Ship	Completion Date	Builder
SD NEWHAVEN	2000	Aluminium SB
SD NUTBOURNE	2000	Aluminium SB
SD NETLEY	2001	Aluminium SB

(A2¾2) —

Tonnage 77 tonnes (45 grt) **Dimensions** 18.3m x 6.8m x 1.88m **Speed** 10 knots **Complement** 2/3 Crew (60 passengers)

Notes

MCA Class IV Passenger Vessels acquired as replacements for Fleet tenders. Employed on general passenger duties within the port area. To remain in service until 2022. SD NETLEY and SD NUTBOURNE are based at Portsmouth, SD NEWHAVEN is based at Devonport and operates in support of Flag Officer Sea Training (FOST). Has undergone modifications to strengthen her forward bollard and add transfer wings to enable under-way personnel transfers with some classes of vessel undertaking sea training. Utilised if SD CAWSAND, SD BOVISAND or SD OBAN are out of service or unavailable.

SD Padstow

PADSTOW CLASS

Ship	Completion Date	Builder
SD PADSTOW	2000	Aluminium SB

Tonnage 77 tonnes (45 grt) **Dimensions** 18.3m x 6.8m x 1.88m **Speed** 10 knots
Complement 2/3 Crew (60 passengers)

Notes

MCA Class IV, VI and VIA Passenger Vessel based at Devonport. Used on liberty runs
in Plymouth Sound and the Harbour as well as occasionally supporting FOST. Has
undergone similar modifications as SD NEWHAVEN (previous page) in order to conduct
underway personnel transfers. To remain in service until 2022.

OBAN CLASS

Ship	Completion Date	Builder
SD OBAN	2000	McTay Marine
SD ORONSAY	2000	McTay Marine
SD OMAGH	2000	McTay Marine

G.R.T 199 tons **Dimensions** 27.7m x 7.30m x 3.75m **Speed** 10 knots **Complement** 4 Crew (60 passengers)

Notes

MCA Class IIA Passenger Vessels which replaced Fleet tenders in 2001. SD OBAN was transferred to Devonport in 2003 and is now primarily used to support FOST staff. SD ORONSAY and SD OMAGH employed on general passenger duties on the Clyde and are additionally classified as Cargo Ship VIII(A). To remain in service until 2022.

SD Norton

PERSONNEL FERRY

Ship	Completion Date	Builder
SD NORTON	1989	FBM Marine

G.R.T 21 tons **Dimensions** 15.8m x 5.5m x 1.5m **Speed** 13 knots **Complement** 2

Notes

The single FBM catamaran, 8837, operated at Portsmouth. Can carry 30 passengers or 2 tons of stores. Was a prototype catamaran designed to replace older Harbour Launches but no more were ordered.

• JOHN CRAE

SD Eva

PERSONNEL FERRY

Ship	Completion Date	Builder
SD EVA	2009	Damen

G.R.T 168 tons **Dimensions** 33.21m x 7.4m x 3.3m **Speed** 23.4 knots **Complement** 4-6 (plus 34 passengers)

Notes

Operated on the Clyde as a Fast Crew Transport. The Axe Bow design allows the vessel to effectively cut through waves with minimal movement of the vessel. The vessel is the first of its type in the UK to be operated under the International Code of Safety for High Speed Craft (HSC Code).

SD Menai

FLEET TENDERS

Ship	Completion Date	Builder
SD MELTON	1981	Richard Dunston
SD MENAI	1981	Richard Dunston
SD MEON	1982	Richard Dunston

G.R.T. 117.3 tons **Dimensions** 24m x 6.7m x 3.05m **Speed** 10.5 knots **Complement** 4 (12 passengers)

Notes

The last three survivors of a once numerous class of vessels used as Training Tenders, Passenger Ferries, or Cargo Vessels. MENAI and MEON are operated at Falmouth. MELTON is operated at Kyle of Lochalsh. A vessel replacement programme now seems unlikely and this elderly trio are expected to remain in service until 2022.

SD Teesdale

COASTAL OILER

Ship	Completion Date	Builder
SD TEESDALE	1976	Yorkshire Drydock Co.

G.R.T. 499 tons **Dimensions** 43.86m x 9.5m x 3.92m **Speed** 8 knots **Complement** 5

Notes

Formerly the oil products tanker TEESDALE H operated by John H Whitaker. Operates as a parcel tanker delivering diesel and aviation fuel and also delivering / receiving compensating water. She is self propelled by two Aquamaster thrusters.

A Diesel Lighter Barge, SD OILMAN, and a Water Lighter Barge, SD WATERPRESS, are operated on the Clyde. A further barge, a Liquid Mixed Lighter Barge, SD OCEANSPRAY, is based at Portsmouth.

SD Northern River

MULTI-PURPOSE VESSEL

Ship	Completion Date	Builder
SD NORTHERN RIVER	1998	Myklebust (Norway)

G.R.T 3,605 tons **Dimensions** 92.8m x 18.8m x 4.9m **Speed** 14 knots **Complement** 14

Notes

Bought from Deep Ocean AS (a subsidiary of Trico Marine) this Ulstein UT-745L designed Support Vessel entered service with Serco in March 2012. She can be employed on a variety of tasking from target towing, through noise ranging to data gathering; boarding training to submarine escort. Her extensive flat work deck allows her to embark containers for passive sonar training. She can also provide nuclear emergency support as well as support to submarine emergencies. She can provide mother ship training facilities for the NATO Submarine Rescue System (NSRS), which involves the embarkation, fitting and operation of specialist ROV's, escape vessels and Transfer Under Pressure (TUP) facilities on the after deck, together with the embarkation of up to 40 additional personnel. She can also support the Submarine Parachute Assistance Group.

SD Moorhen

DIVING SUPPORT VESSELS
MOOR CLASS

Ship	Completion Date	Builder
SD MOORFOWL	1989	McTay Marine
SD MOORHEN	1989	McTay Marine

Y 33

Y 32

Displacement 518 tons **Dimensions** 32m x 11m x 2m **Speed** 8 knots **Complement** 10

Notes

Designed as a powered mooring lighter for use within sheltered coastal waters the lifting horns have been removed from the bows of both vessels when they were converted to Diving Support Vessels. They are used by the Defence Diving School for diving training in the Kyle of Lochalsh. To remain in service until 2022.

87

SD Navigator

MULTICAT 2510 CLASS

Ship	Completion Date	Builder
SD NAVIGATOR	2009	Damen, Hardinxveld
SD RAASAY	2010	Damen, Hardinxveld

G.R.T 150.27 tonnes **Dimensions** 26.3m x 10.64m x 2.55m **Speed** 8 knots
Complement 3 (plus up to 12 additional personnel)

Notes

SD NAVIGATOR is equipped for buoy handling with a single 9 ton capacity crane. She is capable of supporting diving operations. SD RAASAY is based at the Kyle of Lochalsh. She is fitted with two cranes for torpedo recovery and support diving training. SD NAVIGATOR is managed from Portsmouth, but operates between Devonport and Portsmouth. Two similar vessels, SD INSPECTOR (ex-DMS EAGLE) and SD ENGINEER operate from Portsmouth and Devonport respectively.

SD Angeline

MULTICAT 2613S CLASS

Ship	Completion Date	Builder
SD ANGELINE	2015	Damen, Gorinchem

G.R.T 200 tonnes **Dimensions** 26.25m x 13m x 3.7m **Speed** 10.1 knots **Complement** Accommodation for 8 persons, consisting of four double crew cabins

Notes

Her total power output is 2,850 kW with a bollard pull of 45 tons. The crane has a capacity of 15 tm. Ordered April 2014 Accepted by the MoD in April 2015 although there are still operational trials to take place. Built at the request of the MoD to provide support in Faslane Naval Base primarily to Submarines.

SD Solent Racer

STAN TENDER 1505 CLASS

Ship	Completion Date	Builder
SD CLYDE RACER	2008	Damen, Gorinchem
SD SOLENT RACER	2008	Damen, Gorinchem
SD TAMAR RACER	2008	Damen, Gorinchem

G.R.T 25.19 tonnes **Dimensions** 16m x 4.85m x 1.25m **Speed** 20 knots **Complement** 3 (+ 10 Passengers)

Notes

Of aluminium construction these boats are employed on transfer of pilots, port security operations and passenger and VIP transportation.

SD Solent Spirit

STAN TENDER 1905 CLASS

Ship	Completion Date	Builder
SD CLYDE SPIRIT	2008	Damen, Gorinchem
SD SOLENT SPIRIT	2008	Damen, Gorinchem
SD TAMAR SPIRIT	2008	Damen, Gorinchem

G.R.T 43.3 tonnes **Dimensions** 18.91m x 5.06m x 1.65m **Speed** 21.7 knots **Complement** 3 (+ 10 passengers)

Notes

Steel hull with aluminium superstructure. Special propeller tunnels are fitted to increase propulsion efficiency and to reduce vibration and noise levels. These vessels are able to operate safely and keep good performance in wind speeds up to Force 6 and wave heights of 2 metres. Employed on transfer of pilots, VIPs and personnel.

Kingdom of Fife

ANCHOR HANDLING TUG

Ship	Completion Date	Builder
KINGDOM OF FIFE	2008	Damen, Galatz

Displacement 1,459 tons **Dimensions** 61.2m x 13.5m x 4.75m **Speed** 13.7 knots **Complement** 18

Notes

Briggs Marine won a £100m contract from Serco to support navigation buoy maintenance and mooring support for the Royal Navy for 15 years. During the contract period, Briggs Marine provide support for over 350 moorings, navigation buoys and targets
for the RN all around the UK coast, as well as Cyprus, Gibraltar and the Falkland
Islands. KINGDOM OF FIFE was delivered in May 2008 and supports the existing
Briggs Marine shallow draught and heavy lift craft CAMERON in servicing the contract,
and is equipped with a decompression chamber and its own dedicated dive support
team.

Smit Towy

AIRCREW TRAINING VESSELS

Ship	Comp Date	Builder	Base Port
SMIT DEE	2003	BES Rosyth	Buckie
SMIT DART	2003	BES Rosyth	Plymouth
SMIT DON	2003	BES Rosyth	Blyth
SMIT YARE	2003	FBMA Cebu	Great Yarmouth
SMIT TOWY	2003	FBMA Cebu	Pembroke Dock
SMIT SPEY	2003	FBMA Cebu	Plymouth

G.R.T. 95.86 GRT **Dimensions** 27.6m x 6.6m x 1.5m **Speed** 21 knots **Complement** 6

Notes

The service for Marine Support to Ranges and Aircrew Training is provided by SMIT (Scotland) Ltd and runs until April 2017. These vessels provide training for military aircrew in marine survival techniques, helicopter winching drills, target towing and general marine support tasks. More recently they have participated in Navy Command boarding exercises, simulating arms and drug smuggling activities and force protection exercises involving both Fast Attack Craft and Fast Inshore Attack Craft. SMIT DART completed as a passenger vessel with a larger superstructure. A smaller, second-hand vessel, SMIT TAMAR is employed in a similar role.

Smit Stour

RANGE SAFETY VESSELS

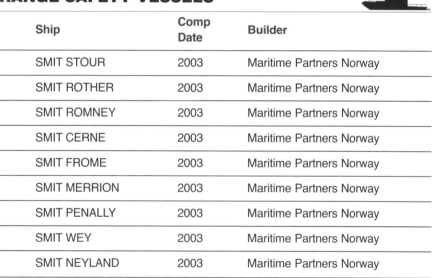

Ship	Comp Date	Builder
SMIT STOUR	2003	Maritime Partners Norway
SMIT ROTHER	2003	Maritime Partners Norway
SMIT ROMNEY	2003	Maritime Partners Norway
SMIT CERNE	2003	Maritime Partners Norway
SMIT FROME	2003	Maritime Partners Norway
SMIT MERRION	2003	Maritime Partners Norway
SMIT PENALLY	2003	Maritime Partners Norway
SMIT WEY	2003	Maritime Partners Norway
SMIT NEYLAND	2003	Maritime Partners Norway

G.R.T. 7.0 tons **Dimensions** 12.3m x 2.83m x 0.89m **Speed** 35 knots **Complement** 2

Notes

A class of 12 metre Fast Patrol Craft which operate on Range Safety Duties at Dover, Portland and Pembroke.

94

AWB Diablo

ARMY VESSELS
WORK BOATS

Vessel	Pennant Number	Completion Date	Builder
STORM	WB41	2008	Warbreck Eng.
DIABLO	WB42	2008	Warbreck Eng.
MISTRAL	WB43	2008	Warbreck Eng.
SIROCCO	WB44	2008	Warbreck Eng.

Displacement 48 tonnes **Dimensions** 14.75m x 4.30m **Speed** 10 knots
Complement 4

Notes

Part of the Army's strategic port operations in Southampton, but can be transported by a 'mother ship' to other ports and places like Iraq. Are often used as tugs for mexeflotes, positioning other pontoon equipment and for handling flexible pipelines. They have a fire-fighting capability. The Army also operate a number of smaller Combat Support Boats. Built by RTK Marine/VT Halmatic (now BAE) these are fast and rugged small craft, 8.8m long with a twin Hamilton waterjet propulsion system powered by twin 210hp diesel engines.

HMC Seeker

BORDER FORCE
STAN PATROL 4207 CLASS

Vessel	Pennant Number	Completion Date	Builder
SEARCHER	-	2002	Damen
SEEKER	-	2001	Damen
VALIANT	-	2004	Damen
VIGILANT	-	2003	Damen

Displacement 238 GRT **Dimensions** 42.8m x 7.11m x 2.52m **Speed** 26+ knots
Complement 12

Notes

These vessels are able to remain at sea for extended periods and in heavy weather conditions. They operate 24 hours a day, 365 days per year, through the employment of dual crews. There are ten crews for the five Border Force cutters comprising 120 seagoing staff, working two weeks on and two weeks off. Cutters are mostly deployed on a risk-led or intelligence-led basis detecting prohibited and restricted goods, boarding and searching ships and providing a law enforcement presence in remote and inaccesible areas. Vessels are prefixed HMC for Her Majesty's Cutter. The are recognised by a diagonal blue, white, red, white stripe on the bows. All five cutters are now based at Portsmouth.

HMC Protector

TELKKÄ CLASS

Vessel	Pennant Number	Completion Date	Builder
PROTECTOR	-	2002	UKI Workboat

Displacement 400 tonnes **Dimensions** 49.7m x 7.5m x 3.9m **Speed** 22 knots
Complement 12

Notes

Acquired in 2013 she is the former Finnish Border Agency vessel TAVI. From May 2014 PROTECTOR, together with HMC SEEKER, was deployed to the Mediterranean to conduct search and rescue operations and help in tackling the criminal gangs that are responsible for illegal attempts to move large numbers of migrants across the Mediterranean. They worked alongside the Royal Navy, the Royal Marines and other agencies as part of Operation Triton, led by Frontex, the EU's external border control agency. During the five-month deployment, the two vessels were stationed at Catania, Sicily and Taranto, Italy. During this period Border Force officers saved more than 1,650 lives and intercepted 26 suspected people smugglers who were handed over to authorities in Italy.

AIRCRAFT OF THE FLEET AIR ARM

During 2016 there will be increasingly significant changes in the way the Fleet Air Arm deploys aircraft at sea, maintains them and delivers operational capability.

Tailored Air Groups or TAGs began to replace standardised air groups after 2006 when the Sea Harrier was prematurely withdrawn from service. Rather than complete squadrons forming a designated air group, aircraft carriers now embark small detachments only 'when needed' for specific exercises or operations and with only one big-deck ship in commission, OCEAN, sea time is at a premium. QUEEN ELIZABETH will be able to embark TAGs comprising F-35B Lightning IIs, Merlin HM2 and HC4 together with Wildcats, Apaches and Chinooks but sources in the US Navy have expressed concern that the MOD plans to stage a 'maximum effort' carrier-based deployment with 24 F-35Bs embarked in one of the two new carriers only once every two years as part of the UK carrier generation cycle. At other times smaller numbers will be embarked to maintain operational skills.

Aircraft maintenance is achieved through international and joint projects, each with a different UK project team at Abbey Wood backed by its own industrial grouping and software. The British F-35B in VMFAT-501 is maintained in accordance with US Navy regulations and not the UK Military Regulatory Publication although the Lightning Project Team at Abbey Wood has responsibility for its airworthiness. Maintenance procedures are digital and accessed through the Autonomous Logistics Information System, ALIS managed by Lockheed Martin. The Merlin HM2 and Wildcat also use integrated digital technical publications, with no paper manuals, managed by AgustaWestland and overseen by the Merlin and Wildcat Project Teams, also at Abbey Wood. The F-35 and Wildcat use 'on condition' maintenance techniques with serviceability determined by on-board health monitoring systems which detect faults and even damage. The introduction of these disparate regimes and the need for their software administration will have a major impact on TAG management and technician training in the immediate future and are bound to affect career patterns and advancement.

Gaps in aircraft numbers have become pronounced as front-line aircraft have been withdrawn before their replacements reach operational maturity. F-35Bs are expected to be delivered at the rate of about 4 a year from 2016 making it unlikely that 24 deployable, operational aircraft for any 'maximum effort' will be available before 2022 at the earliest. Project 'Crowsnest' will deliver an embarked ASaC capability, which is good, but shared use of the 30 Merlin HM2 airframes reduces the number of anti-submarine assets available. The Commando Helicopter Force has at last got a Sea King HC4 replacement but the 20 Merlin HC4s needed to equip the two squadrons will not be available until 2020. By then it will have taken 21 years to fulfil the original SDR decision to replace the Sea King and the Merlins that do so will be refurbished rather than new.

AIRCRAFT & SQUADRONS

Squadron	Aircraft	Page
700X	SCANEAGLE	107
703	TUTOR T1	109
705	SQUIRREL HT1	110
727	TUTOR T1	109
736	HAWK T1	101
750	AVENGER T1	108
809	F-35B LIGHTNING II (forming)	100
814	MERLIN HM2	102
815	WILDCAT HMA2/LYNX HMA8	104/105
820	MERLIN HM2	102
824	MERLIN HM2	102
825	WILDCAT HMA2	104
829	MERLIN HM2	102
845	MERLIN HC3/3i	103
846	MERLIN HC3/3i	103
847	WILDCAT AH1	104
849	SEA KING ASaC7	106
VMFAT-501	F-35B LIGHTNING II	100
17 (Joint)	F-35B LIGHTNING II	100
617 (Joint)	F-35B LIGHTNING II (forming)	100
DAUPHIN Flight	DAUPHIN 2	111
RNHF	SWORDFISH	
	SEA FURY	
	SEA HAWK	
	SEA VIXEN	
	CHIPMUNK	112

Lockheed Martin F-35B LIGHTNING II

Role Strike, fighter and reconnaissance aircraft
Engine 1 X Pratt & Whitney F135-PW-600 delivering 41,000lb thrust with reheat in conventional flight; 40,650lb hover thrust with Rolls-Royce lift fan engaged and tail nozzle rotated.
Length 51' 4"   **Wingspan** 35'   **Height** 15'
Max Weight 60,000lb **Max Speed** Mach 1.6 **Crew** 1 pilot
Avionics AN/APG-81 AESA radar; AN/AAQ-40 electro-optical targeting system; AN/AAQ-37 distributed aperture system; AN/ASQ-239 'Barracuda' electronic warfare system; pilot's helmet-mounted display system; multi-function advanced data link.
Armament Current Block 2B software allows the stealthy carriage of weapons in 2 internal bays with a single ASRAAM or AMRAAM air-to-air missile plus a single 1,000lb bomb equivalent such as Paveway IV LGB in each. Block 3F software in operational aircraft delivered from 2016 will enable the additional use of 7 non-stealthy external pylons, 3 under each wing and 1 under the centreline. A total of 12,000lb of weapons or fuel tanks to be carried; inner wing pylons have 'plumbing' for 426 US gallon drop tanks.
Squadron Service VMFAT-501, 17 Squadron, 617 Squadron (forming within VMFAT-501).

Notes
The only British aircraft to have an American, rather than British, type designation and mark number, reflecting the international nature of its support software. 17 Squadron is a joint unit with 35 RN and 35 RAF personnel at Edwards AFB. VMFAT-501, 'Warlords', at MCAS Beaufort has an RN AEO plus 6 technicians and an RAF pilot plus 7 technicians. RN and RAF personnel for the first British operational unit, 617 Squadron, are training within VMFAT-501. It is due to have 12 aircraft and 240 personnel, split 50% between the RN and RAF, when it moves to the UK in August 2018. 809 Squadron is expected to train and begin to form within VMFAT-501 at MCAS Beaufort about a year behind 617, moving to the UK during 2020.

BAE Systems HAWK T 1

Role Role Operational training and threat simulation aircraft
Engine 1 x Rolls Royce Adour 151 delivering 5,200lb of thrust.
Length 40' 9" **Wingspan** 32' 7" **Height** 13' 1"
Max Weight 20,000lb **Max Speed** Mach 0.88 (Mach 1.2 in a dive) **Crew** 1 or 2 pilots
Avionics standard communications fit
Armament Can be fitted with a 30mm gun pod on a centreline pylon and one pylon under each wing capable of taking AIM-9 Sidewinder or up to 1,500lb of practice weapons

Squadron Service 736 Naval Air squadron

Notes
736 NAS is the focus for fast-jet expertise within the RN command structure. It has responsibility for flying standards, lead-in training for newly-qualified RN pilots destined to fly the F-35B Lightning II and provides continuity flying for RN pilots who have returned from flying USN and French strike fighters. 736 NAS also provides aircraft for fighter controller and ASaC observer training and attack simulations for FOST activities and 'Joint Warrior' exercises, effectively acting as an RN 'aggressor unit'. The aircraft are maintained by Babcock under contract and the squadron usually operates in two flights, one each at RN Air Stations Yeovilton and Culdrose. Under current plans the Hawk T 1 is due to be withdrawn from service in 2020 and potential replacement aircraft are being considered.

AgustaWestland MERLIN HM2

Role Anti-submarine search and strike; maritime surveillance
Engines 3 x Rolls Royce/Turbomeca RTM 322 each developing 2,100 shp
Length 74' 10" **Rotor diameter** 61' **Height** 21' 10"
Max Weight 32,120lb **Max Speed** 167 knots **Crew** 1 or 2 pilots, 1 observer, 1 air-crewman
Avionics Blue Kestrel radar; Orange Reaper ESM; Folding Light Acoustic System for helicopters (FLASH); AQS-903 acoustic processor; Wescam MX-15 electro-optical/IR camera; defensive aids including Directional Infrared Countermeasures (DIRCM), AN/AAR-57 radar warning system, chaff and flare dispensers;
Armament Up to 4 Stingray torpedoes or Mark 11 depth charges; 1 x M3M 0.5" machine-gun in cabin door and 1 x 7.62mm machine-gun in cabin window

Squadron Service 814, 820, 824, 829 Naval Air Squadrons

Notes
814 and 820 NAS provide TAG detachments in OCEAN and RFAs, 829 NAS provides single aircraft flights for some frigates and 824 NAS is the type's training and tactical development unit. They are shore-based at RNAS Culdrose and all 30 Merlin HM 2s are expected to be modified by 2018 to enable them to be fitted, optionally, with the palletised Cerberus mission system under project 'Crowsnest' as an alternative to the anti-submarine avionics, allowing them to be used for either A/S or ASaC missions as required for TAG deployments and training. 10 'Crowsnest' systems are to be procured with 7 or 8 aircraft fitted at any one time for operation with 849 NAS leaving the remaining sets as a contingency reserve. 12 Merlin HM 1s remain in storage and are being stripped as a source of spare parts.

STEVE WRIGHT

AgustaWestland MERLIN HC3, HC3i and planned HC4

Role Commando assault, load-lifting, troop movement
Engines 3 x Rolls Royce/Turbomeca RTM 322 each developing 2,100 shp
Length 74' 10" **Rotor diameter** 61' **Height** 21' 10"
Max Weight 32,120lb **Max Speed** 167 knots **Crew** 1 or 2 pilots, 1 aircrewman
Avionics Wescam MX-15 electro-optical/IR camera; defensive aids suite including directional IR countermeasures, AN/AAR-57 missile approach warning system, automatic chaff and flare dispensers
Armament 1 x M3M 0.5" machine-gun in cabin door; 1 x 7.62mm machine-gun in cabin window

Squadron Service 845, 846 Naval Air squadrons.

Notes
25 Merlin HC3s were transferred from the RAF to replace the Sea King HC4 in the RN Commando Helicopter Force, CHF, and moved to RNAS Yeovilton in 2015. 7 have been modified to HC3i standard, allowing embarked operation and have power-folding main rotor heads, taken from stored HM1s, lashing points and better communications. All 25 are to be modified to HC4 standard with a glass cockpit similar to the HM2, power-folding main rotor heads and folding tail pylons but the last is not due to be completed until 2022. Eventually, the two squadrons are each to have 10 aircraft with 845 NAS maintaining three deployable flights and 846 NAS an operational conversion flight, a maritime counter-terrorism flight and a deployable flight to back up 845. The remaining 5 aircraft will be used as attrition reserves.

STEVE WRIGHT

AgustaWestland WILDCAT AH1, HMA2

Roles Surface search and strike; anti-submarine strike; boarding party support (HMA 2); reconnaissance and troop movement (AH 1)
Engines 2 x LHTEC CTS 800 each developing 1,362 shp
Length 50' **Rotor diameter** 42' **Height** 12'
Max Weight 13,200lb **Max Speed** 157 knots **Crew** 1 pilot & 1 observer
Avionics Selex-Galileo Sea Spray 7400E multi-mode AESA radar; Wescam MX-15 electro-optical/IR camera; Electronic warfare system and defensive aids suite. Bowman communications system
Armament 2 x Stingray torpedoes or Mark 11 depth charges; 1 x M3m 0.5" machine-gun in cabin door. From 2020 to carry Martlet (light) and Sea Venom (heavy) air-to-surface guided weapons.

Squadron Service 815, 825, 847 Naval Air squadrons

Notes
847 NAS operates the AH1 version in the tactical reconnaissance role as part of the CHF. 825 NAS is the Wildcat HMA2 training and tactical development unit and 815 NAS deploys operational flights to destroyers, the frigates that do not embark Merlins and some RFAs. The Wildcat is not a 'Lynx upgrade' but an entirely new aircraft built round a digital avionics management system designed to enhance mission effectiveness and reduce aircrew work-load. Delays in procuring the Martlet and Sea Venom air-to-surface guided weapons, however, mean that the Wildcat will not achieve its intended strike capability until at least 2020. All three squadrons are shore-based at RNAS Yeovilton.

AgustaWestland LYNX HMA8

Roles Surface search and strike; anti-submarine strike; boarding party support
Engines 2 x Rolls Royce Gem BS 360-07-26 each developing 900 shp
Length 39' 1" **Rotor diameter** 42' **Height** 11'
Max Weight 9,500lb **Max Speed** 150 knots **Crew** 1 pilot & 1 observer
Avionics Sea Spray radar; Orange Crop ESM system; Sea Owl electro-optical/Infrared camera; SATURN communications system
Armament Up to 4 Sea Skua air-to-surface missiles or 2 Stingray torpedoes or 2 x Mark 11 depth charges. 1 x M3M 0.5" machine gun in cabin door and 1 hand-held Heckler & Koch G 3 sniper rifle to support boarding parties.

Squadron Service 815 Naval Air Squadron

Notes

A small number of Lynx remain in service while 815 NAS completes its conversion to the Wildcat. The last of these is due to be retired in March 2017, partially filling the gap before the Martlet and Sea Venom air-to-surface guided weapons reach initial operational capability with the Wildcat. When the last Lynx is withdrawn, the type will have been in operational service with the RN for forty years, since 1977. 702 NAS, the former Lynx training unit was stood down in 2014.

AgustaWestland SEA KING ASaC7

Role Airborne Surveillance and Control
Engines 2 x Rolls Royce Gnome H 1400 each developing 1,600 shp
Length 54' 9" **Rotor diameter** 62' **Height** 17' 2"
Max Weight 21,400lb **Max Speed** 125 knots **Crew** 1 pilot and 2 observers
Avionics Cerberus mission system; Searchwater radar; Orange Crop ESM; Link 16; AN/AAR-57 missile approach warning system; IR jammer; radar warning receiver; automatic chaff and flare dispenser
Armament none

Squadron Service 849 Naval Air Squadron

Notes

The last Sea Kings in service with the RN, 7 Sea King ASaC7s are to be retained until 2018 when the Merlin HM2/Crowsnest system is due to achieve initial operational capability. 849 NAS fills a training and tactical development role and is shore-based at RNAS Culdrose. It supports two operational flights named 'Normandy' and 'Palembang' after 2 of the unit's battle honours, each capable of deploying as part of a TAG. The Sea King first went into service with the RN with 700S NAS in 1969 and all other variants were withdrawn from service on 31 March 2016. The UK SAR task formerly undertaken by 771 NAS was taken over by civilian contractors.

Boeing SCANEAGLE

Role Unmanned surface search and reconnaissance
Engine 1 x Sonex heavy fuel (JP 5), pusher, piston engine developing 0.97KW
Length 5' 1" **Wingspan** 10' 3" **Height** 2'
Max Weight 48.5lb **Max Speed** 80 knots
Avionics EO900 electro-optical/IR imagers in a nose-mounted turret; analogue, digitally-encrypted control link; encrypted video downlink
Armament None

Squadron Service 700X Naval Air Squadron

Notes

ScanEagle operating units are provided by Boeing under a 'contractor owned and operated' deal with the MoD although each detachment has an RN safety officer trained to 'fly' the air vehicle. They are deployed in selected frigates and RFAs in addition to manned helicopters to provide the parent ship's command team with real-time reconnaissance images out to 70 miles from the parent vehicle for up to 18 hours. The air vehicle is launched from a portable pneumatic catapult and is recovered by catching a vertical wire attached to the launcher unit with hooks on its wingtips. It is 'flown' throughout the mission by a pilot at a console in the parent ship's operations room. 700X NAS is based at RNAS Culdrose and is also tasked with giving advice on the procurement and deployment of unmanned air vehicles. AgustaWestland has been contracted to evaluate both unmanned and optionally-manned helicopters for the RN.

OTHER AIRCRAFT TYPES IN ROYAL NAVY SERVICE

Beech AVENGER T1

Role Observer training
Engines 2 x Pratt & Whitney PT6A-60A, each developing 1,050 shp
Length 46' 8" **Wingspan** 57' 11" **Height** 14' 4"
Max Weight 15,000lb **Max Speed** 313 knots
Crew 1 or 2 pilots, 4 student observers plus instructors
Avionics Surface search and ground mapping radar
Armament None

Squadron Service 750 Naval Air Squadron

Notes

750 NAS operates 4 Avengers as part of the Observer School at RNAS Culdrose to provide the third phase of the training syllabus. The first two phases are flown with 703 NAS at RAF Barkston Heath. The third phase lasts for 7 months and includes classroom work and simulator exercises as well as flying.

GROB TUTOR T1

Role Elementary training
Engine 1 x Textron Lycoming AE10-360-B1F developing 180 shp
Length 24' 9" **Wingspan** 32' 9" **Height** 7'
Max Weight 2,178lb **Max Speed** 185 knots **Crew** 2 pilots
Avionics None
Armament None

Squadron Service 703, 727 Naval Air Squadrons

Notes

703 NAS forms part of the Defence Elementary Flying Training School at RAF Barkston Heath. It has a naval commanding officer, senior pilot and flying instructors but the aircraft are maintained under civilian contract. It trains about 50 naval students a year including both pilots and observers. 727 NAS at RNAS Yeovilton carries out the flying grading of newly-entered RN and RM aircrew and other light fixed-wing tasks. It also offers an introductory 'look' at naval flying for civilians interested in a flying career with the Royal Navy. Aircraft are maintained by Babcock who also provide 5 flying instructors to supplement the RN commanding officer, training officer and a variable number of RNR flying instructors.

LEE HOWARD

Eurocopter SQUIRREL HT1

Role Basic helicopter training
Engine 1 x Turbomeca Ariel 2D developing 847 shp
Length 35' **Rotor diameter** 36' **Height** 9' 3"
Max Weight 5,225lb **Max Speed** 155 knots **Crew** 2 pilots plus up to 5 passengers
Avionics None
Armament None

Squadron Service 705 Naval Air Squadron

Notes

705 NAS forms part of the Defence Helicopter Flying School at RAF Shawbury, teaching basic helicopter handling, instrument flying, low flying and other skills to students from all three UK armed forces and some Commonwealth countries. It has an RN commanding officer and senior pilot who provide a naval focus within the school but the other instructors are drawn from the Army and RAF as well as the RN.

Eurocopter AS365N DAUPHIN 2

Role Passenger movement and training support
Engines 2 x Turbomeca Arriel 2C each developing 838 shp
Length 39' 9" **Rotor diameter** 39' 2" **Height** 13' 4"
Max Weight 9,480lb **Max Speed** 155 knots **Crew** 1 or 2 pilots plus up to 11 passengers
Avionics None
Armament None

Notes

Similar to the H-65 helicopters operated by the US Coast Guard, 2 of these civil-owned military-registered, COMR, helicopters are operated for the RN by Bond Helicopters under contract. They are based at Newquay airport and used to support FOST in the sea areas off Plymouth. They are commonly tasked to transfer passengers between ships at sea but can also undertake a wide variety of other roles. A new helicopter operating facility has been built within Devonport Naval Base from which FOST staff can be flown from their headquarters directly to ships at sea.

Royal Navy Historic Flight

Notes

Based at RNAS Yeovilton, the Flight includes Swordfish I W 5856; Swordfish II LS 326; Sea Fury FB 11 VR 930; Sea Fury T 20 VX 281; Sea Hawk WV 908 and Chipmunk T 10 WK 608. They are flown in displays by naval pilots and maintained by civilians under a MoD contract but are seldom all serviceable at the same time.

In September 2014 the last airworthy Sea Vixen FAW 2, XP 924, was handed over to the Fly Navy Heritage Trust at RNAS Yeovilton. It will be operated alongside the aircraft of the RN Historic Flight.

STEVE WRIGHT

AGUSTAWESTLAND APACHE AH 1

Notes Army Air Corps Apaches can be armed with up to 16 AGM-114 Hellfire missiles or up to 76 CRV-7 unguided rocket projectiles plus a single M230 30mm cannon with 1,160 rounds. Operated as part of the Joint Helicopter Force.

CROWN COPYRIGHT/MoD 2015

BOEING CHINOOK

Notes RAF Chinooks are able to carry up to 44 fully equipped troops or a 20,000lb load and are armed with miniguns to give suppressive fire in assault landings. Operated as part of the Joint Helicopter Force.

WEAPONS OF THE ROYAL NAVY

Sea Launched Missiles

Trident II D5

The American built Lockheed Martin Trident 2 (D5) submarine launched strategic missiles are Britain's only nuclear weapons and form the UK contribution to the NATO strategic deterrent. 16 missiles, each capable of carrying up to 6 UK manufactured thermonuclear warheads (but currently limited to 4 under current government policy), can be carried aboard each of the Vanguard class SSBNs. Trident has a maximum range of 12,000 km and is powered by a three stage rocket motor. Launch weight is 60 tonnes, overall length and width are 13.4 metres and 2.1 metres respectively.

Tomahawk (BGM-109)

This is a land attack cruise missile with a range of 1600 km and can be launched from a variety of platforms including surface ships and submarines. Some 65 of the latter version were purchased from America to arm Trafalgar class SSNs with the first being delivered to the Royal Navy for trials during 1998. Tomahawk is fired in a disposal container from the submarine's conventional torpedo tubes and is then accelerated to its subsonic cruising speed by a booster rocket motor before a lightweight F-107 turbojet takes over for the cruise. Its extremely accurate guidance system means that small targets can be hit with precision at maximum range, as was dramatically illustrated in the Gulf War and Afghanistan. Total weight of the submarine version, including its launch capsule is 1816 kg, it carries a 450 kg warhead, length is 6.4 metres and wingspan (fully extended) 2.54 m. Fitted in Astute & T class submarines. It was announced in 2014 that the US Navy are to stop procuring the missile in 2015 which has implications for the production line, although an MoD spokesman expected this not to impact on UK requirements. In July 2014 the UK requested 65 missiles to replace those expended on coalition operations. In September 20 Block IV missiles were ordered.

Harpoon

The Harpoon is a sophisticated anti-ship missile using a combination of inertial guidance and active radar homing to attack targets out to a range of 130 km, cruising at Mach 0.9 and carrying a 227 kg warhead. It is powered by a lightweight turbojet but is accelerated at launch by a booster rocket. Fitted to Type 23 frigates and four Type 45 destroyers.

Sea Viper (Aster 15/30)

Two versions of the Aster missile will equip the Type 45 Destroyer, the shorter range Aster 15 and the longer range Aster 30. The missiles form the weapon component of the Principal Anti Air Missile System (PAAMS). Housed in a 48 cell Sylver Vertical Launch system, the missile mix can be loaded to match the ships requirement. Aster 15 has a range of 30 km while Aster 30 can achieve 100 km. The prime external difference between the two is the size of the booster rocket attached to the bottom of the missile. PAAMS is known as Sea Viper in RN service.

Sea Wolf

Short range rapid reaction anti-missile missile and anti-aircraft weapon. The complete weapon system, including radars and fire control computers, is entirely automatic in operation. Type 23 frigates carry 32 Vertical Launch Seawolf (VLS) in a silo on the foredeck. Basic missile data: weight 82 kg, length 1.9 m, wingspan 56 cm, range c.5-6 km, warhead 13.4 kg. The VLS missile is basically similar but has jettisonable tandem boost rocket motors.

Sea Ceptor

Incorporating the Common Anti-Air Modular Missile (CAAMM) family, being developed to replace the Rapier and Seawolf SAM systems, plus the ASRAAM short range Air-to-Air Missile. It will arm the Royal Navy's Type 23 frigates and its Type 26 Global Combat Ships. In Spring 2012 the MoD awarded MBDA UK a five-year Demonstration Phase contract worth £483 million to develop the missile for the RN. In September 2013 a £250 million contract was announced to manufacture the missile in the UK, sustaining around 250 jobs at MBDA sites in Stevenage, Filton and Lostock. Installation of the Sea Ceptor on Type 23 frigates started in 2015 with ARGYLL and the last will be completed by 2021. CAMM missiles will be fitted in the existing VL Seawolf silo (one canister per cell for a maximum of 32 missiles).

Air Launched Missiles

Sea Skua

A small anti-ship missile developed by British Aerospace arming the Lynx helicopters carried by various frigates and destroyers. The missile weighs 147 kg, has a length of 2.85 m and a span of 62 cm. Powered by solid fuel booster and sustainer rocket motors, it has a range of over 15 km at high subsonic speed. Sea Skua is particularly effective against patrol vessels and fast attack craft, as was demonstrated in both the Falklands and Gulf Wars.

Guns

114mm Vickers Mk8 Mod 1

The Royal Navy's standard medium calibre general purpose gun which arms the Type 23 frigates and Type 45 destroyers. The Mod 1 is an electrically operated version of the original gun and is recognised by its angular turret. First introduced in 2001 it is now fitted in all Type 23 and Type 45 vessels. Rate of fire: 25 rounds/min. Range: 22,000 m. Weight of Shell: 21 kg.

Goalkeeper

A highly effective automatic Close in Weapons System (CIWS) designed to shoot down missiles and aircraft which have evaded the outer layers of a ships defences. The complete system, designed and built in Holland, is on an autonomous mounting and includes radars, fire control computers and a 7-barrel 30 mm Gatling gun firing 4200 rounds/min. Goalkeeper is designed to engage targets between 350 and 1500 metres away. However, with the decommissioning of the BIII Type 22 frigates and the carrier ILLUSTRIOUS there remains just the two mounts on the operational LPD. As a result the RN has determined to discontinue support for the system after 2015 and it is likely that during ALBIONs regeneration refit the system will be removed and replaced by either Phalanx or a more conventional close in systems. The same will happen to BULWARK when she enters refit in 2016.

Phalanx

A US built CIWS designed around the Vulcan 20 mm rotary cannon. Rate of fire is 3000 rounds/min and effective range is c.1500 m. Fitted in Type 45, OCEAN and some Wave, Bay and Fort classes. Block 1B began entering service from 2009. Incorporates side mounted Forward looking infra-red enabling CIWS to engage low aircraft and surface craft. In October 2012 it was announced that a further five Phalanx Block 1B mountings were to be procured to protect RFA ships.

DS30B 30mm

Single mounting carrying an Oerlikon 30mm gun. Fitted to Type 23 frigates and various patrol vessels and MCMVs. In August 2005 it was announced that the DS30B fitted in Type 23 frigates was to be upgraded to DS30M Mk 2 to include new direct-drive digital servos and the replacement of the earlier Oerlikon KCB cannon with the ATK Mk 44 Bushmaster II 30 mm gun. Consideration is already being given to purchasing additional DS30M Mk 2 systems for minor war vessels and auxiliaries.

GAM BO 20mm

A simple hand operated mounting carrying a single Oerlikon KAA 200 automatic cannon firing 1000 rounds/min. Maximum range is 2000 m. Carried by most of the fleet's major warships except the Type 23 frigates.

20mm Mk.7A

The design of this simple but reliable weapon dates back to World War II but it still provides a useful increase in firepower, particularly for auxiliary vessels and RFAs. Rate of fire 500-800 rounds/min.

Close Range Weapons

In addition to the major weapons systems, all RN ships carry a variety of smaller calibre weapons to provide protection against emerging terrorist threats in port and on the high seas such as small fast suicide craft. In addition it is sometimes preferable, during policing or stop and search operations to have a smaller calibre weapon available. Depending upon the operational environment ships may be seen armed with varying numbers of pedestal mounted General Purpose Machine Guns (GPMG). Another addition to the close in weapons is the Mk 44 Mini Gun a total of 150 of which have been procured from the United States as a fleetwide fit. Fitted to a naval post mount, the Minigun is able to fire up to 3,000 rounds per minute, and is fully self-contained (operating off battery power).

Torpedoes

Sting Ray

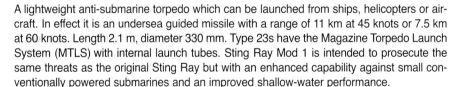

A lightweight anti-submarine torpedo which can be launched from ships, helicopters or aircraft. In effect it is an undersea guided missile with a range of 11 km at 45 knots or 7.5 km at 60 knots. Length 2.1 m, diameter 330 mm. Type 23s have the Magazine Torpedo Launch System (MTLS) with internal launch tubes. Sting Ray Mod 1 is intended to prosecute the same threats as the original Sting Ray but with an enhanced capability against small conventionally powered submarines and an improved shallow-water performance.

Spearfish

Spearfish is a submarine-launched heavyweight torpedo which has replaced Tigerfish. Claimed by the manufacturers to be the world's fastest torpedo, capable of over 70 kts, its sophisticated guidance system includes an onboard acoustic processing suite and tactical computer backed up by a command and control wire link to the parent submarine. Over 20ft in length and weighing nearly two tons, Spearfish is fired from the standard 21-inch submarine torpedo tube and utilises an advanced bi-propellant gas turbine engine for higher performance. To undergo a £270 million upgrade which will include a new warhead, a chaange to the fuel system to improve safety, full digitisation of the weapon and a new fibre optic guidance link to improve performance. The work is to be carried out by BAE Sytems at Portsmouth with deliveries beginning in 2020 and continuing to 2024.

Future Weapons

Sea Venom

Formerly known as the Future Anti-Surface Guided Weapon (Heavy), Sea Venom is high-subsonic 'drop-launch' missile in the 110 kg-class incorporating an imaging infrared seeker (with provisions for an additional semi-active laser guidance channel), a two-way datalink for operator-in-the-loop control, and a 30kg warhead. Designed by MBDA to replace the helicopter air-launched Exocet, the missile will have a range of up to 25 km and will be able to counter targets up to corvette size. The FASGW programme, comprising both Heavy and Light missiles, is a joint venture between the UK and France. The missile will equip the RNs Wildcat helicopter and, in July 2014, AgustaWestland received a £90 million contract to integrate the respective variants for deployment from the Wildcat HMA2. Each aircraft will be able to carry four missiles and it is anticipated that Initial Operating Capability will be achieved in 2020, although there are aspirations that this date will move left.

Martlet

Formerly known as the Future Anti-Surface Guided Weapon (Light), this missile is designed to counter small boat and fast inshore attack craft threats. It is based on the laser beam-riding variant of the Thales Lightweight Multi-role Missile (LMM). With a range of up to 8 km it carries a 3 kg blast fragmentation/shaped charge warhead travelling at about Mach 1.5. Missiles will be carried in a five-round launcher (with each Wildcat able to carry up to four launchers). Alternatively a mix of two Sea Venom on the outer pylon and two five round Martlet on the inner weapons station can be carried. An active laser guidance unit integrated within the L-3 Wescam nose turret will support laser beam-riding guidance. Trials of both variants of FASGW are planned to take place between late 2018 to late 2019.

At the end of the line ...

Readers may well find other warships afloat which are not mentioned in this book. The majority have fulfilled a long and useful life and are now relegated to non-seagoing duties. The following list gives details of their current duties:

Pennant No	Ship	Remarks
D23	BRISTOL	Type 82 Destroyer - Sea Cadet Training Ship at Portsmouth.
M29	BRECON	Hunt Class Minehunter - Attached to the New Entry Training Establishment, HMS RALEIGH, Torpoint, as a static Seamanship Training Ship.
M103	CROMER	Single Role Minehunter - Attached to BRNC, Dartmouth as a Static Training Ship.
L3505	SIR TRISTRAM	Refitted as a Static Range Vessel at Portland.
S50	COURAGEOUS	Nuclear-powered Submarine - On display at Devonport Naval Base. Can be visited during Base Tours. Tel: 01752 552326 for details.
C35	BELFAST	World War II Cruiser Museum ship - Pool of London. Open to the public daily. Tel: 020 7940 6300
D73 S17	CAVALIER OCELOT	World War II Destroyer & Oberon class Submarine Museum Ships at Chatham. Open to the public. Tel: 01634 823800
S67	ALLIANCE	Submarine - Museum Ship at Gosport Open to the public daily. Tel: 023 92 511349
LCT7074	LANDFALL	A D-Day veteran. Refloated in October 2014 six years after she sank at Birkenhead. Undergoing restoration by the NMRN at Portsmouth.
M1115	BRONINGTON	The ship remains at Birkenhead, in poor condition, whilst discussions over its future continue.
	BRITANNIA	Ex Royal Yacht at Leith. Open to the public.
	CAROLINE	Light Cruiser and veteran of the Battle of Jutland. Is to be restored and opened as a tourist attraction at Belfast in time for the 2016 Battle of Jutland centenary.
	M33	Coastal Monitor and veteran of the Gallipoli Campaign on display at Portsmouth as part of the National Museum of the Royal Navy.

STEVE WRIGHT

The Batch III Type 42 destroyer YORK leaving Portsmouth under tow of tug DIAVLOS PRIDE on 18 August 2015 bound for recycling.

At the time of publishing (December 2015) the following ships were laid up in long term storage or awaiting sale.

PORTSMOUTH: Illustrious; Endurance; Walney.

PLYMOUTH: Tireless; Trafalgar; Turbulent; Sceptre; Superb; Splendid; Spartan; Sovereign; Conqueror; Valiant; Warspite.

ROSYTH: Resolution; Renown; Repulse; Revenge; Swiftsure; Churchill; Dreadnought.

Since the previous edition the following vessels in long term storage or awaiting scrap were disposed of:

EDINBURGH: Departed Portsmouth under tow of tug SPARTAN on 12 August 2015 bound for recycling at Leyal Shipbreakers, Turkey.

YORK: Departed Portsmouth under tow of tug DIAVLOS PRIDE on 18 August 2015 bound for recycling at Leyal Shipbreakers, Turkey.

GLOUCESTER: Departed Portsmouth under tow of tug HELLAS on 22 September 2015 bound for recycling at Leyal Shipbreakers, Turkey.